There are stories in these old mountains, and Lynn Coffey knows how to tell them. Stories, like music, get passed down from generation to generation. And like the tunes from a fiddle or banjo, Lynn's words echo and resonate through Appalachia.

—Tommy and Yvette Stafford,
Nelson County Life magazine

Backroads 3

Faces of Appalachia

Lynn Coffey

Cover design by Jane Hagaman
Front cover art by Lynn Coffey, Owen Garfield Campbell/Montebello
Back cover art, Faces of Appalachia collage, by Lynn Coffey
Author photograph by Bob Nelms
Interior design by Jane Hagaman
Unless noted, all interior photos by Lynn Coffey

Quartet Books
PO Box 4204
Charlottesville, VA 22905

If you are unable to order this book from your local
bookseller, you may order directly from the author.
Call (540) 949-0329 or use the order form in the back
of the book. For more information about all three of
the Backroads books, you may browse Lynn's website
at www.backroadsbooks.com.

Library of Congress Control Number: 2011930540

ISBN 978-0-615-49310-7
10 9 8 7 6 5 4 3 2 1
Printed on acid-free paper in USA

*Dedicated to the sweet faces and giving hearts of the mountain people,
whom I love and defend with everything in me*

Faces of Appalachia

Contents

Foreword

If you want to know something of the love the mountain folk have for their neighbor Lynn Coffey, then just look into their faces.

A very early form of photography employed a copper plate that had been prepared with an application of silver and mercury. The fragile plate was exposed inside a camera box when the shutter was opened, capturing an exact image of the subject on the shiny surface. Today, looking at those miraculously produced images is like looking over the shoulder of the subjects as they peered at themselves in a mirror.

Likewise, reading the Backroads stories is akin to tagging along with Lynn Coffey and watching over her shoulder as she shares time with her Appalachian neighbors. Their faces reflect Lynn's sweet spirit of love and a genuine appreciation of them as God's creations. Emanating from their visages is their trust and appreciation for this woman who was an outsider among them for only a short while.

Lynn hungered to learn their rapidly disappearing ways of living, not simply to obtain a façade of fitting in, but so she could genuinely adapt their experiences and wisdoms into her own life. Her neighbors' acknowledgment of her sincerity was manifested in many forms, the most important of which was by their inclusion of her in their day-to-day activities.

While making a living from the land—planting, nurturing, protecting, harvesting, preserving—the good seasons as well as the difficult ones showed in the strength of their hands, the resilience of their spirits, and the lines of their faces. With her camera at the ready, Lynn preserved moments of their lives that remind us today of what rural life was like only a generation ago.

The source of Lynn Coffey's strong spirit and devotion is her unmistakable faith in God. She could no more ignore the greatest holy commandment to love her Lord than she could the second greatest, which is to love her neighbor. In 1981, her love for her neighbors took on the form of a small monthly newspaper that she published for the next twenty-five years.

Visits on the mountain, visits in the valleys. Home visits, garden visits, hospital visits, funeral-home visits. Making notes, taking pictures, shaping storylines, typing, cutting, pasting, folding, and delivering. Soliciting advertisements, taking subscriptions, maintaining the books. Month after month, year after year.

The Backroads newspaper was Lynn's vehicle for loving her neighbors by honoring and affirming their lives on the printed page. Her task was not without many bittersweet moments, though, as one by one through the years, many of her much-beloved neighbors passed on to their eternal reward. All the while, the rest of us simply sat back and rustled through the pages to learn the latest stories and gaze upon a continual showing of faces and places and thingamajigs.

Now the Backroads volumes take the place of many of those saved newspapers and yellowed clippings—yet another blessing from Lynn. So, savor the visits. Don't be so hasty to read too much at once. Look over the writer's shoulder, and study the faces. Relish being allowed to tag along.

—Phil James

Phil James is the author of the book *Secrets of the Blue Ridge* and a newspaper column by the same name, which appears in the *Crozet Gazette*. He and his wife, Sally, live in the Blue Ridge Mountains of central Virginia. They can testify to the pleasant comforts of the Coffey's rocking chairs and the deliciousness of Lynn's homemade apple pies.

Acknowledgments

Once again, I am indebted to those special folks who made the Backroads series possible. Without them, I could never imagine undertaking writing one book about the Appalachian culture, much less three. It has been a joy compiling the old stories from *Backroads* newspaper and putting them in book form. My heartfelt thanks to each person who helped make the Backroads books a reality.

First and foremost, I humbly thank God for giving me the talent for writing and the love of the mountain people and the old ways that have been with me from the beginning. He also blessed me with a German heritage; probably the reason I stubbornly stuck to the business of single-handedly publishing a newspaper for twenty-five years when people told me I couldn't do it. He gave me my gift and told me to go use it. I'm so glad I did!

Next I'd like to thank my husband, Billy, for being the most patient and selfless man I've ever met. He knew when he married me that he'd be inheriting not only a bride but also a newspaper. He's been my most ardent supporter during the time I've written three books and wasn't above scrubbing the floors or doing dishes while I was sequestered at my desk, pawing through mountains of paper. If it weren't for his computer skills and electronic expertise, I'd be sunk. Technology is not my forte!

For the girls of Quartet Books, who took a chance on an unknown author, putting my work into legible print and making me and the books look highly professional. It was my lucky day when I made that first phone call and hired them to put everything together. Thanks again, girls, for all your hard work.

Special thanks to all the accomplished authors who were generous enough to write glowing forewords and beautiful endorsements for all three books. They say it's what's written on a book's cover that makes people want to pick it up. Your kind words helped to convey the message of the Appalachian culture in its most positive light.

For the endearing mountain people who shared their lives, families, and histories with a virtual outsider from the flatlands of Florida, so she could use her God-given talent to bring honor to the very ones who made all her dreams come true. There are no adequate words to say how much love my heart holds for you, but through the pages of *Backroads*, I hope you'll know.

Introduction

Well. This is it. I find myself sitting here having mixed emotions about writing one last introduction to the Backroads book series. It has been such a journey, writing three books in two years about the vanishing culture of Appalachia. In thumbing through all the old Backroads newspapers to pick subject matter for the book, I am again reminded that most of the people I interviewed from 1981 through 2006 are now gone. All those dear faces etched in my mind and words imbedded in my heart have become so entwined with my own life that I cannot tell one from the other. I only know I miss them.

All I ever wanted was to move to the mountains and learn enough of the old ways to live a simplistic lifestyle. God not only made my childhood dream come true, but He also tapped into some hidden talents I never knew I possessed. Writing down my thoughts and taking photographs was always a big part of who I am. Like the proverbial five loaves and two fishes, God took the few things He blessed me with and multiplied them into a feast, with baskets and baskets of leftovers. I am living proof that He can use anybody for anything if they are but willing.

In twenty-five years of publishing *Backroads* newspaper and two years spent writing books, I admit to the fact I still have no idea what I'm doing. That alone tends to keep one humble. Over the years, I have learned a lot but continue to be totally dependent on my Lord to keep me on track, lest I stray off course. I tell anyone who will listen that God has a perfect plan for each of His children, and all they have to do is ask what He wants them to do, listen to what He says, and then do it. If you're faithful in using your gift, everyone gets the blessing. Years ago, when I was discouraged enough to quit the newspaper, someone sent me a little piece that snapped me to attention, made me pull myself up by the boot-straps, and start again. It is entitled "Do Your Work," and I am including it in case there's a person reading this who is as discour-aged as I was and needs courage to move forward.

> Keep about your work that God has given you. Do not flinch because the lion roars; do not stop to stone the devil's dogs; do not fool away your time chasing the devil's rabbits. Do your work. Let liars lie, let corpora-tions resolve, let the devil do his worst; but see to it that nothing hinders you from fulfilling the work that God has given you.
>
> He has not commanded you to get rich. He has never bidden you to defend your character. He has not set you at work to contradict falsehoods about yourself which Satan and his servants may start to peddle. If you do those things, you will do nothing else; you will be at work for yourself and not for the Lord.
>
> Keep at your work. Let your aim be as steady as a star. You may be assaulted, wronged, insulted, slandered, wounded, and rejected; you may be abused by foes, for-saken by friends, and despised and rejected of men. But see to it with steadfast determination, with unfaltering zeal that you pursue the greatest purpose of your life and object of your being until at last you can say . . .
>
> "I have finished the work which Thou gavest me to do."

In *Plain Folk and Simple Livin'* and *The Road to Chicken Holler*, I chose just a few personal interviews and mixed them in with the activities and crafts of the mountain people. In *Faces of Appalachia*, I turn the tables and showcase more personal interviews instead of the activities. I did it this way to include as many of the elder folks as possible. In our area of the Blue Ridge, everyone seems to be kin, so if one person was featured, whole families took credit for their words and history. Even so, I still didn't have space to put each one I would have liked, but I tried to represent a few from each community around Love.

As I retyped stories from the newspaper for the book, I began to notice similarities in all the interviews. God, family, hard work, and thankfulness were the common threads woven into the fabric of every person's memory. Life centered on God and worship because it was believed the only thing standing between them and certain death was God's grace. Families pulled together and worked hard but still made time for a bit of fun along the way. The mountain people didn't have much in the way of material things, but they were rich in the things that mattered and were thankful for the little they did have. But along with the similarities, each had their own experience and twist on life that made reading their stories interesting and memorable.

People like Ora Robertson, who at two years of age was given to a neighboring family by her father because her mother had run away, and Ora was too young to work in the fields. At seven she was stolen back from the family that raised her when her father deemed she was old enough to hoe corn.

Or Hallie Henderson, a gritty little woman widowed at thirty-two who went to work on the night shift at a blanket factory to make enough money to raise her three little boys by herself. She rose early to a full load of housework, cooking, laundry, and baths, all without the convenience of electricity or indoor plumbing.

The younger generation needs to be told about the hardships their ancestors faced and how they rose above these hardships to live happy, productive lives.

Today I had an experience that left me full of emotion and wondering at the odd twist my own life has taken. I went down to Maynard Patterson's house in Sherando to return the photographs he had lent me for the chapter written about his brother, Gordon. As we talked, Maynard asked me questions about events that had happened years ago, long before I was born. I answered him with the knowledge gleaned from the older mountain people who had talked to me over the years. The conversation went back and forth like that for perhaps a half hour before I left.

Later that evening, the emotion of that conversation hit me full force. I nearly wept, telling Billy, "I was answering questions about an era in which I never lived and talking about people I never knew, only they weren't my memories . . . they were theirs." Through the telling, the people and places of yesteryear have come to life and are real in my mind. I am the vessel these memories travel through, giving them voice. The thought nearly broke me, and I asked Billy why the mountain people entrusted *me* to pass on their sacred stories. His answer touched me deeply: "It's where your heart is. . . ."

Backroads 3

Gladys Coffey at her seventy-fifth birthday celebration

1

Gladys Elizabeth Taylor Coffey

Love and Reed's Gap, Virginia

Every now and then, one is blessed with a special friend whose very life and everyday actions give the world a glimpse of what heaven must be like. I am honored to know such a woman and have always regarded her as part of my own family, long before I inherited that privilege by marriage. I can't put down in mere words what she actually means to me or the impact her life has had on my heart, so I will share some of the memories of Gladys that are the dearest to me.

I met Gladys Coffey and her family a few years before moving to the Love community and immediately knew I'd hit it off with her, although there was an age difference of twenty-five years between us. She had what you'd call an "all around" personality; devoted wife to husband, Boyd, loving mother to her four children, and a doting grandmother/great-grandmother.

To give you a little of Gladys's early history, I will start at the beginning of her life.

Gladys Elizabeth Taylor was the first of four daughters and one son born to William and Lillian Cook Taylor in Falls Church, Virginia, on August 17, 1922. Her brother, William Irvin, died in infancy, but she and her three sisters—Edna, Irene, and Anna—grew up on the family farm, helping with all the chores. Gladys's father was a lumberman who worked for the Murphy-Ames Lumber Company, and her gentle mother, Lillian, was a homemaker and raised the children.

Gladys attended first and second grade at the Falls Church
Grammar School and when she was nine years old, the family
moved to Oakton, Virginia, where she finished elementary school.
Back then the elementary schools consisted of classes from the first
through seventh grades, and if a young person wanted more education, she had to attend the high school in Fairfax that supplied
grades nine through eleven. When Gladys was fourteen, she
skipped a year of school to live with her aging grandparents, helping them with their daily activities. After that year, an aunt and
uncle came to live with the grandparents. Thus started Gladys's
long career of taking care of others in the family.

She graduated from high school at eighteen and at nineteen,
began dating a boy by the name of Boyd Coffey, whose family was
then living in Alexandria. Boyd originally began dating Gladys's
sister Edna, but after two dates he realized it was Gladys he was
meant to be with. They dated for about a year and then had a two-
month engagement before marrying on August 28, 1941.

Mr. Taylor had given his daughter an acre of land on which the
young couple had planned to build a house. The first year, they
built an eighteen-by-twenty-four-foot garage, which they could
live in until they could finish a house. In the meantime, Mr. Taylor had an offer on his entire farm, and asked Gladys if she would
consider selling her acre for $1,000 along with the rest of the prop-
erty. Gladys said she felt like this was a fortune, so she and Boyd
sold their land and moved to Falls Church.

During the year they had lived in Oakton, the couple's first
daughter, Betty, was born, and in the fall of 1942, they bought their
house in Falls Church. They lived there for twenty-eight years,
and their other three children—Carol Jean, Judy, and Roger—
were born and raised there. During that time, the Coffey's took in
several other relatives who lived with them for a while.

Boyd was an auto mechanic, and he and Gladys ran their own
business in Falls Church. After all the children were grown and
gone, the Coffeys had one year together before Boyd's father, Wallace, passed away. Wallace and his family were living in Love, Virginia, at that time, and the decision was made to move to the

remote mountain community to take care of Boyd's mother and his two mentally handicapped brothers, Samuel and Harvey, who still lived at home.

Boyd and Gladys moved to Love in September 1968 and began taking on the care and welfare of another whole family. In spite of this huge responsibility, Gladys managed to maintain her own unique, independent spirit. I never heard her complain about moving from the comforts of city life to an isolated farm in the Blue Ridge Mountains, even when her mother-in-law became an invalid and needed constant care. Eventually, Harvey went to live with Boyd's sister, Nellie Umbarger, but Samuel continued to live with Gladys, even after Boyd passed away in December 1993, until his own death in 1997.

Gladys in 1980 at the Love homeplace

Gladys and her brother-in-law Samuel

When I moved to Love, Gladys was a constant amazement to me, with her many skills ranging from fine carpentry to delicate stitching of colorful quilts. There was nothing she couldn't do. One day I went over to her house to find Gladys taking out the small living room window and replacing it with a large picture window she'd scrounged from somewhere. Another time she decided to move an entire staircase that led upstairs, and she did it so fast that her husband didn't notice it for days. Gladys is one of the few women I know who was positively thrilled when, one Christmas, her son-in-law Chuck gave her her own toolbox.

Countless times she accompanied me on interviews for *Backroads* newspaper and rode with me each month to deliver the papers. Oh the fun we had, cruising down gravel roads to secluded cabins where people were waiting to tell us about their early lives.

Over the years, I was the proud recipient of many birthday and anniversary cakes, decorated with her signature brightly colored icings. She sent cards to the sick, made visits to the shut-ins, and offered words of encouragement to those going through rough times. She was the taker-in of strays, of which I was one. She always signed her cards to me, "To my fifth child . . . from your second Mom."

Two of the funniest memories I have while living in Love included Gladys. I told her for our first Christmas here that I wanted a very tall tree, since the hunting camp where we lived had a cathedral ceiling. Gladys said there were some tall blue spruce trees on their Reed's Gap property and we'd go look for one. The trees ended up being much too tall, so she suggested climbing halfway up one enormous spruce and topping it. We both shinnied up the trunk, hanging on for dear life as the tree swayed back and forth as I cut the top off with a hand saw. We dragged the greenery home, and it was still so tall that we had to cut it four more times before it would fit inside the cabin. I remember I had to stand on a step ladder to decorate it.

Another time she called me on a snowy February morning, asking if I'd meet her on the same piece of Reed's Gap property to dismantle an old barn. Never having engaged in this type of activity before, I was curious as to how a couple of women were going to manage this feat. She just told me to pack a lunch, bring a crowbar, and meet her over there in fifteen minutes. That cold winter day I learned one of Gladys's key bywords in life: Never underestimate the power of a woman! Within two hours, Gladys and I and our neighbor Bunny Stein, who had also been recruited, had the barn down and its lumber stacked in neat little piles where the barn had stood. I felt proud to have been a part of such an accomplishment, and I learned firsthand that there was practically nothing that my friend couldn't do once she set her mind on it.

Yet with all her determination and strength, Gladys Coffey is one of the most feminine, humble, and submissive women I ever met. She is an everyday lesson in Christian compassion and kindness, giving God credit for all she does and is able to do. And like Ruth and Naomi in the Bible, I'd follow Gladys anywhere.

Gladys's eightieth birthday with her children (L—R: Carol Jean, Betty, Roger, and Judy)

Gladys on her eightieth birthday with the family

After Boyd's mother passed away, and Boyd retired from Baugher Chevrolet in 1984, the Coffey's decided to move from the homeplace in Love over to Reed's Gap, where they undertook the large project of building their own house. Both were in their sixties at the time. They moved into their new home in 1986, and it was a big celebration for the whole family. That home became the hub for all holiday parties, as well as impromptu get-togethers that always seemed to involve music and food.

Mountain-woman fashionista

Gladys's kind, patient nature is partly from her gentle upbringing but mostly because she is a woman of great faith. Many years ago, Gladys made the decision to be a follower of Jesus Christ and once that decision was made, she never looked back to her old life. Her faith has been a constant through the good times and the bad, maturing her into a "Proverbs 31" woman, tenfold. She is a living example of how God wants us to act toward our fellow man, showing love to everyone, especially to those embittered and unloving. There must have been times when I disappointed Gladys and let her down, but there was never a mention of my unthoughtful ways, only unconditional love.

So this first chapter in *Backroads 3: Faces of Appalachia* is dedicated to and honors an exceptional woman by the name of Gladys Elizabeth Taylor Coffey . . . my second Mom.

Portions taken from the October 1997
and August 2004 *Backroads*

Ceclia Powell; Waynesboro, Virginia

Samuel Coffey at his Love, Virginia, homeplace

2

Samuel Robert Coffey

Love and Reed's Gap, Virginia

Samuel Robert Coffey was born to Wallace and Martha Goode Coffey on March 8, 1929. Immediately after birth, it was apparent that Sam was mentally handicapped, yet over the years, he was the one who taught us all great lessons in unconditional love and acceptance of oneself and others.

Sam, along with his brother Boyd and sister-in-law Gladys, was one of the first people I met in the Love community before actually moving here.

The first thing that struck me most about Samuel was his brilliant cornflower-blue eyes. Those eyes, along with his outgoing personality, stood out with such clarity that you forgot he was a little different.

One of the funniest memories I have of myself is a photograph that was taken of me and Sam standing in the middle of Reed's Gap when it was still a dirt road. Boyd and Gladys were having a big get-together on their property over there, and everyone was taking pictures, so I suggested one be taken of Sam and me. While the photographer fiddled endlessly with the right camera setting, Samuel had literally put the squeeze on me, hugging tighter and tighter until I thought I'd pass out from lack of breath or plain fear. Sam enjoyed nothing better than giving a woman a tight embrace . . . a *long* tight embrace! When the film was developed, I had a good laugh over that moment caught by the camera. Sam's face was illuminated with an enormous smile of happiness while mine had a trapped animal look; eyes wide open, looking for a way out.

That was many years ago, and somewhere along the way, Sam's hugs and hearty handshakes were not only to be expected but looked forward to by all his friends. His voice and high-pitched laugh are forever imprinted in our minds, along with the assorted greetings he reserved for each of us.

Lynn and Sam in 1981

Another memory of Samuel I will always treasure, and one which never fails to give me a good laugh, is the time he scared some New York tourists out of their wits. Someone had given Sam a silver sheriff's badge, and he loved flashing it around to unsuspecting people. One morning my daughter missed the school bus, and we raced down the mountain in the car to catch up with it at Marcie Hatter's house, whose lane was right next to the Coffey's. Between us and the bus was another vehicle with New York license plates. They had to stop for the bus as the children boarded, and Sam took advantage of that moment to approach the tourists. The woman on the passenger side of the car rolled down the window about the same time Sam started talking gibberish and flashing his sheriff's badge. The window was promptly rolled back up and the vehicle took off, passing the bus in record time! I laughed all the way home. Shortly thereafter, Samuel's badge was confiscated, putting him out of the sheriff business permanently.

I remember Gladys telling me that after church on Sundays, Samuel would head for the woods to find a tree stump on which to stand and "preach" sermons loud and long to a make-believe congregation.

One thing about Samuel, he definitely knew how to enjoy life and take pleasure in the simple things around him. To him, everyone was special, and he always made you feel that way. He accepted you totally. I can honestly say that in the many years I knew him, I never saw him without his signature smile.

When his brother Boyd passed away in December 1993, Sam continued to live with Gladys at their home on Reed's Gap, and he attended every function that was held at church, at friend's homes, or family get-togethers. I remember one Forth of July party we held at our cabin. Sam helped turn the crank on the homemade ice-cream maker and enjoyed several big bowls of peach ice cream for his efforts.

Early in 1997, we all began to notice that Sam was coughing a lot. Gladys took him to the doctor, thinking it was just a case of bronchitis. But the coughing continued, and an MRI was done, revealing a large tumor in Sam's chest. Within a two-month period, Samuel had become a shadow of his

Sam with a bear that his hunting party got in 1984

former self, and it was deemed necessary for him to undergo surgery and a few radiation treatments to save his life. But his recovery was not meant to be, and those of us who loved him had to say goodbye and let him go. It wasn't an easy thing to do because Sam was one of those special people who stood out in life and in everyone's memory.

August 12, 1997, was a sad and unexpected day for a lot of folks who'd had the privilege of knowing Samuel Robert Coffey. For it

was on this day that Sam's spirit quietly slipped away to be reunited
with many of his family members and friends who had made the
same journey years before. He died quietly at home, and Gladys
said that just before his passing, Sam kept pointing at something
across the room, making excited gestures and sounds and smiling
this huge smile. No one in the room could see what Sam was
pointing at, but as he gently slipped away, Gladys felt God had
sent an angel or allowed a deceased family member come back to
accompany Samuel to heaven.

During the sad time of his death, I heard a lot of uplifting stories from Sam's friends. They were happy memories of a man who
loved everyone in his own unique way and left his mark upon their
hearts.

Emmie Gibson, our former mail carrier, recalled how Samuel
would stop all traffic, including VDOT workers, to make sure
Emmie could maneuver her little green Volkswagen to the mailbox. She also laughed at the memory of Sam sheltering her under
an umbrella on rainy Sunday's at Waynesboro Mennonite Church
where they attended, leaving her husband, David, to dodge the
rain by himself.

Orvin Kiser, Sam's Sunday-school teacher and good friend, said
he never knew a person more willing than Samuel to do any task
asked of him.

Orvin's wife Phyllis commented on the little stuffed toys people had brought to him in the hospital. When asked if he enjoyed
them, Gladys said he enjoyed the *people* who brought him the gifts
more than the actual toys.

William Hatter, a younger neighbor and friend of the Coffey's
who grew up around Samuel, spoke at his funeral, saying things
that touched everyone in attendance. He told how Sam never
seemed to age despite his sixty-eight years of living and how as
children they both started out with pure and tender hearts. "Somehow, as I grew up, I lost my innocence, but Sammy continued to
have a pure heart until the day he died."

Stanlee Kauffman, pastor of Waynesboro Mennonite Church,
said Sam taught us some valuable lessons in the way God wants us

to live a victorious life. "He didn't dwell on his handicaps but accepted and loved himself just as God made him. And because he could accept himself, he could accept others with an unconditional love that is rarely found in today's world. He was a willing servant in church and in life, always putting others first."

On and on the testimonials went, with people standing to recite personal stories about how Samuel had positively affected them over the years. I wept openly at the loss of one so dear to us all. How ironic that a man with no money of his own turned out to be one of the richest men the world has ever seen. I suddenly realized how short of the mark we fall; how Samuel Robert Coffey was the perfect one, and we are the ones struggling with all kinds of handicaps.

Sam's niece, Judy Akers, said it so eloquently when she spoke of her Uncle Sam. "Isn't it funny that the world doesn't pay that much attention to people who are doing big things in life? It's people like Sam, who are a little bit different, that we take notice of. They are the ones who have the most impact on our lives."

Judy also wrote a thank-you letter to her mother's church for the kindness everyone extended to the Coffey family during Sam's illness. In it, she shared her views about her uncle. I wanted to include her words because I felt they reflected Samuel's life through the eyes of his own family.

Sam was a sixty-eight-year-old uneducated, retarded, gentle man who had no idea of his limitations. He never held a job, never drove a car, and never operated any type of machine. He faced each day with enthusiasm, a bright smile, and a warm handshake. He wore no teeth, nor would he wear his glasses. Finding fault or complaining was not a part of his life. Uncle Sam could tell time on the hour and half hour and lived on a schedule of rising by six o'clock in the morning, feeding his dog and cats, putting water on for coffee, and then walking the floor until Gladys would arise and fix his breakfast by eight o'clock. He knew he would then eat lunch when both hands on the watch were straight up. He loved hot dogs. He knew when the truckers would by passing by his home and would be

on the porch to wave and get them to blow their horn for
him. He was the keeper of the keys to the house, garage,
and outbuildings and was always ready to assist in opening doors. Posing for a picture by himself or with another
was a treat and privilege. Sam's life was busy, purpose-
ful, meaningful, unconditional, free of guilt, and he never
met a stranger or forgot a face. Samuel Coffey was a true
example of God's love.

As the closing words at Sam's funeral were being said, my husband Billy nudged me to look at a large banner hanging from the
church wall. The words inscribed on it were a fitting end as we
prepared to say a final goodbye to a very special friend.

"Imperfect persons reflecting God's perfect love."

Samuel Coffey brightened our little corner of the world with a
taste of what God's perfect love really is: total acceptance and
unconditional love. What greater legacy can a man leave behind?

Taken from the October 1997 *Backroads*

Jim and Vi Courtney; Love, Virginia

Chestnut trees growing at the Sloan farm in Massies Mill

3

The American Chestnut Tree

Early Uses and the Blight That Killed It

There were a variety of trees that were extremely useful to the early mountain people. White oak was easy to split and thus was used in weaving all types of utility baskets. Red oak and hickory were excellent for keeping the cabin fires hot throughout the long cold nights. But the top choice for the early mountaineers was always the versatile chestnut.

Castanea dentata, or the American chestnut by its common name, was at one time one of the most valuable trees growing in this country. Its range was from southern Maine west to Michigan and south to northern Georgia and Alabama. The tree itself grew straight and tall, often reaching heights of over one hundred feet. The huge diameter of the trunk made for a large timber industry right outside the mountain people's doors. One tree within the Great Smoky Mountains of Tennessee was reported as having a circumference of thirty-three feet at four feet from the ground, which is about ten or eleven feet in diameter. Many other reports of the huge girths were recorded through the years, and a wealth of products were made from the wood itself. Telephone poles could be cut from trees with just fifteen to twenty years' growth.

The wood was light and easy to handle but would last almost indefinitely. That's why you see a lot of the old split-rail fencing still standing along the Blue Ridge Parkway where farms were once located. Some said the wood was so easy to split for railing that a huge log could be made into about one hundred rails in one day with nothing but a white oak maul and some dogwood wedges. The wood was also used for acid wood, pulpwood, crossties, ditch timber, framing, siding, furniture, and firewood.

If that wasn't enough, the rich, sweet nuts it bore were a source of income and food for the people and their farm animals. Wild animals such as bear, deer, turkey, and squirrel were also richly fed on the abundant chestnuts that grew everywhere in the mountains. People gathered the nuts all through the autumn months and either took them home to dry for the winter or sold them on the market to buy shoes, clothing, or staples such as coffee, sugar, and salt. Folks let their livestock openly graze through the woods to fatten them up on the rich chestnuts before butchering time. The women used the nuts in stuffing and also made various breads for the family over the winter. Many can still remember how wildlife was much more plentiful when the chestnut trees were still growing. It was a case of supply and demand. The land could support a lot more animals because of the overabundance of food produced. When the chestnuts started to disappear, so did the game.

A byproduct of the tree was its huge honey crop. In the spring, the trees were covered with light, cream-colored blooms that filled the entire woods with their sweet, heady perfume. The people said that when you looked up onto the mountainsides, every tree looked as if it were a huge potted plant alive with millions of bees swarming over it. People found they could also derive medicines from the chestnut tree. Leaves were boiled down into juice and applied as a wet dressing to swollen ankles and the like. In talking with many of the older men who logged in this area, the word "extract" would invariably pop up in conversation. "Extract" referred to the tannic acid, which was extracted out of the bark of the trees after the logs were taken to the mill.

The list went on and on; with literally hundreds of uses, this one tree made our country prosper, and the mountain people were thankful to have such a valuable resource right in their own backyard, free for the taking.

Chestnuts on the tree still in burr

All that came to an end in 1904 when a blight, which spread westward from New York, attacked the massive trees and started a downhill spiral from which the chestnuts never recovered. Some sources say the blight actually started when a contaminated Chinese chestnut tree was brought over from Asia to be displayed at the New York Zoological Park. The Chinese variety was a carrier of the disease but was not in any danger of being destroyed by it. But the American strain was susceptible, and the blight infested the trees at an alarming rate. No one ever believed that the entire population of American chestnuts would be wiped out. There were just too many of them growing everywhere. But panic soon spread when entire forests were being destroyed right before the people's eyes. Many said you could see the blight in action; killing trees up one ridge and down the other. Various methods were employed to try to stop the disease from spreading, but all they did was merely slow down the problem, not alleviate it.

The blight was a fungus whose spores, spread by wind, birds, and other animals, entered the inner bark of the tree through openings in the outer bark. It penetrated deep and destroyed tissue then cut off the flow of sap and formed cankers in the bark. Eventually, the cankers girdled the trunk of the tree, and the portion above the girdled area died. The blight, for some reason, did not affect the roots, and they continued to live on for many years after the main trunk died, sending forth new shoots each spring, only to have them die off after just a few years.

Whole forests of once-magnificent chestnut trees were now vast wastelands that scarred the land. My neighbor Johnny Coffey said when the moon was shining, the forest looked as if there were hundreds of white skeletons standing in it. These "skeletons" served as a constant reminder to the mountain people of their tremendous loss. One man stated that the death of the mighty chestnuts was "the worst lick the south ever had." Thousands of people who made their living from the chestnut timber openly mourned the tree's demise and the sadness that prevailed when the blight began to happen is still apparent today.

Chestnuts in burr at the home of Bennie and Bev Sloan; Roseland, Virginia

Ever since the blight was first discovered, many methods have come about to control or erase it. Some of these approaches have shown promise, but so far none have met with much success. Much searching has been done to find individual trees that are naturally resistant to the blight and to use them for breeding stock for future timber, but a completely disease-free variety has not been found. Every now and then, a large tree that has somehow managed to avoid the blight will be found, and the nuts are taken to a laboratory where new techniques are tried to develop a new strain. Experimentation continues, and maybe one day in the future our Blue Ridge Mountains will once again bloom with the beauty and abundance of the great American chestnut trees.

Taken from the November 1983 *Backroads*

Dennis Allen relaxing at his home in Stuarts Draft

4

Harold Dennis Allen

Stuarts Draft, Virginia

Born the first child to Eugene "Hoot" Allen and his wife, Ethel Fitzgerald Allen, on July 10, 1921, Dennis, as he was called, grew up with his brothers, Glenn and Maxie, and sisters, Verna and Louise, in a cabin that bordered Dowell's Ridge with the Tye River running about a half mile below the property. He remembers being told that a midwife by the name of Martha Ann Bradley delivered him. There was no medical doctor deep in the mountains where they lived, so people made do with home remedies to treat their illnesses and midwives to deliver their babies.

The cabin where Dennis was born was called the Jack Hatter place, and it later belonged to Grover Allen. When Dennis was six months old, his parents moved to Eugene's father's homeplace and built a home there. Dennis's siblings were born at that homeplace, and that's where all the Allen children grew up.

Dennis recalls many of the neighbors who lived within a half mile of their home: Andy Sorrells, Ed Maddox, Rob Gerald, Leslie Allen, Plez Taylor, and Pug Allen. Although no one could actually see any of the individual homes of these neighbors, Dennis remembers the mountains being full of people from Montebello down past the little community of White Rock.

All of the Allen children went to Mill Creek School and used a path through the woods that took them exactly a half hour to walk. School hours were from nine in the morning until three in the afternoon, and the children's parents sent them out the door at eight thirty and expected them home by three thirty, so there wasn't much time for mischief along the way. Mill Creek had classes to the seventh grade, and Dennis remembers Marie Seaman and Russell Fauber as being two of his teachers.

Dennis's father farmed and cut timber in the mountains for a living. His mother raised the children and took care of the home. Dennis went to work with his father at an early age, learning the logging trade, which would ultimately become his own. Although the family worked hard, they allowed their children time to play and have a bit of fun. Dennis remembers making "gum-wheel wagons" out of rounds

"Hoot" and Ethel Allen with three of their children: (L–R) Louise, Dennis, and Glenn

cut from a gum tree which were attached to a box on which they'd fashioned axles. They could haul little things in it or ride it down the steep hill by their house. Or they would build a playhouse in the woods where they would roast apples or fry a few potatoes. "We liked to get away from the cabin or else there'd be a job to do," laughed Dennis.

Working with his father cutting timber with cross-cut saws was hard work, yet the Allen men loved the independence of working for themselves. Dennis's daddy owned a Model A truck, and they would load the lumber on it and take it to Vesuvius, where they would go to either Mangus's or Seacrest's store to trade it for supplies. The Allen's exchanged timber for necessary items such as coffee, sugar, salt, soda and baking powder, or whatever else they needed.

"We would get a few groceries each time we'd take a load, but back then you didn't need much because we raised everything ourselves. You could grow near about anything in that rocky mountain soil. My mother canned vegetables, or we would bury things like cabbage and potatoes, and they'd keep all winter long. We'd put apples inside a fodder shock to keep them from freezing. People would spread apple slices on a cloth, and put them on a tin roof to dry; putting them out in the morning and bringing them back in before dark. Folks saved their seeds from one year to the next to plant next year's garden. We would string snap beans on a cord and hang them up to dry. They were called 'shuck beans' and tasted good when you cooked them."

Families back then worked hard, but they still managed to save a little time for fun. The entire Allen family is known for making the best bluegrass music this side of heaven. Sundays were set aside for visiting others and setting down to a meal with family or friends. A few folks had battery radios with a wire strung outside to serve as an antenna. On Saturday nights, they'd all gather around and tune in a Nashville station to listen to the Grand Ole

(L–R) Dennis, Glenn, and Hoot Allen playing at a WSVA barn dance in Harrisonburg, Virginia

Opry from eight o'clock in the evening until one o'clock the next morning. Bluegrass greats like Bill Monroe and the Delmore Brothers, as well as many other familiar singers, entertained the people of the Blue Ridge Mountains who tuned in on the airwaves.

The various families along the Tye River attended the Holiness Church, White Rock Christian, or Evergreen Church for Sunday services. Preachers from Buena Vista would come and hold night revival meetings. Dennis remembers how the mountains would glitter from the light of the lanterns that people carried as they walked to the services. Dennis's family mostly attended the Holiness Church, which was closest to their home, but they would go to the other ones when special services were held.

When he was about fifteen years old, Dennis began to have an interest in attending White Rock Christian Church. Her name was Vivian Coffey! He had known Vivian his entire life, and they had the unusual distinction of being born in the same home. When Dennis's family moved out of the old Jack Hatter home

Courtesy of Butch Allen

The Allen family: (back row, L–R) Ethel, Hoot, Dennis, Glenn, and Louise; (front row, L–R) Maxie and Verna

where they rented, Vivian's parents, Clarence and Mae Sorrells Coffey, moved in. Vivian was born just seven months after Dennis. At seventeen and sixteen years of age, respectively, Dennis and Vivian were married at the Nelson County courthouse in Lovingston, Virginia. They came back to live, like many mountain newlyweds, with one set of parents. Dennis and Vivian lived a short time with his parents before building a two-room cabin of their own on the family property. From there they moved to Mill Creek in a home belonging to a relative by the name of Davis Allen, where they paid a monthly rent of one dollar. When they acquired a cow, another dollar was charged for pasturing it out on the property.

Dennis continued to work in timber with his father, as well as hauling wood for Vivian's father, who owned a nearby sawmill. He made $1.25 a day at that time. Later he bought his own truck and went into the logging business for himself, cutting wood from as far away as West Virginia and Highland County, Virginia, and hauling it back to Buena Vista. He owned a 1951 truck on which he could load five cords of wood, three ranks high.

Dennis remembers working with Ed Allen and purchasing a two-man gasoline-powered chainsaw, which was a step up from the old cross cut saws. He said cutting trees was quicker, but the saw was a lot harder to handle. "It took a real man to handle it . . . the saw weighed close to one hundred pounds and had a three-foot bar." Dennis began contracting out as an independent logger for larger companies, such as Illinois and Fitzgerald Lumber Company in Fairfield, Virginia.

The Allen family prospered and bought 120 acres along the Tye River; it had a small house on it built by Melvin Mays. The property was divided into two sixty-acre plats on either side of the river. One by one, Dennis's five children were born in that home: first Peggy, then Ronny, Dale, Lynn ("Butch"), and Sue.

Around 1943, the family decided to move to the Stuarts Draft area where so many of their relatives were now living. They bought an old home and lived in it while a new dwelling was being built around it. When the new home was finished, part of the old one was then torn down. As their children married and left home, most of them moved within seeing distance of their parents. Peggy, who moved to Scottsville, is the farthest away. All of the Allen sons continue working in the logging industry, just like their father and grandfather before them.

Dennis and Vivian

Dennis retired from his logging business when he was sixty years old. About the same time, Vivian retired from her job at the Blue Ridge Christian Home. Their life has been, and continues to be, full. They own a camp near Mill Creek where several of their children have land, too, and much of their time is spent camping on the property. In addition to their five children, the Allens also have nine grandchildren and sixteen or seventeen great-grandchildren (Vivian laughs and says she's lost count!), all of which keep them busy. Dennis still has the old Allis Chalmers HD-3 tractor he started out with, and he says he'd be lost without it. Vivian spends her time piecing colorful quilts together with her sister, Vera Falls.

Their home is warm and inviting, full of family photographs and memorabilia of the past. A handmade rocking chair, an enormous "Home Comfort" wood cook stove in the large country kitchen, and antique oil lamps, which still get used occasionally, dot the interior of the Allen home. Children, grandchildren, and friends pop in and out at any given time, and all are welcome.

Dennis and Vivian live a comfortable life, yet like so many of the mountain people I've interviewed over the years, they are quick to say the old ways were the best ways. When I asked Dennis if he ever dreamed about living back along the Tye River as a child, he said, yes, sometimes he did. His last quote of the visit summed up the way most of the Blue Ridge natives feel in their heart of hearts.

"Sometimes, I wish we could go back and live that way again."

Taken from the August 1999 *Backroads*

Lizzie Wood at her one hundredth birthday celebration

5

Lizzie Wyant Wood

Sugar Hollow, Virginia

On February 19, 2005, the family of Lizzie Wood honored their mother's one hundredth birthday with a celebration held at the Waynesboro Church of the Brethren. The church social hall was filled with well-wishers who came to pay tribute to the special lady who has inspired so many throughout her lifetime.

Lizzie Gertrude Wyant Wood was born on February 20, 1905, the fourth child of Hiram Chapman Wyant and Cornelia Frances James Wyant, who lived in the Sugar Hollow area of Albemarle County, Virginia. The ten Wyant children, from firstborn down, were as follows: Nettie, Lottie, Ollie, Lizzie, Lemuel, Myrtie, Edna, Hattie, Emory, and Ellis. Myrtie died at two months of age after being born with an open heart, but the other nine children lived to adulthood. Lizzie said she could still remember when her sister died; her father placed the little casket on a lazy Susan on top of a table so everyone could view her before burial. "Papa lifted me up so I could see her, and the dimes that were placed on her eyes to keep them shut were too big," recalled Lizzie.

Hiram Wyant and his wife, Cornelia, were gentle people who loved their children, and Lizzie said she had a wonderful childhood. "Papa and Mama were strict but loving, and we knew we had to listen, but that's why we had such a good family. We don't really know how to appreciate our parents until we become a parent ourselves; it is only then we come to know what they sacrificed."

Lizzie's father was one of those rare men who could do nearly anything with his hands. He was such an accomplished blacksmith that people from as far away as Crozet and Charlottesville came to his shop to get their horses shod. Lizzie recalls that as a young girl she had to turn the handle on her father's forge while he fit horseshoes on the animals. He could fix wagon wheels and carve out new wooden spokes, if needed. He was a cobbler and could also whittle intricate things from wood. Lizzie remembers how he carved tiny monkeys and baskets from peach and cherry seeds, and he made a very ornate walking stick in which

Hiram and Cornelia Wyant at their homeplace

he had carved out a number of perfect wooden balls inside the handle that could be manipulated with the fingers.

In addition to his jobs at home, he was also a timber man, cutting large loads of extract wood and saw logs, which he then sold. Lizzie remembered a time when she and her brother Lem helped their father cut a load of chestnut wood. While he was taking it to the mill in Mechum's River, the two children hoisted the crosscut saw together and cut another load by themselves. Lemuel also taught Lizzie how to shoot. She remembers the first time she ever shot a gun. "Lemmie and I were on the porch, and he was trying to show me how to hold it tight against my shoulder, but I thought it would hurt. He told me to hold it tight and aim at a bee's nest attached to the kitchen chimney. I aimed and fired and shot it the first time!"

Lizzie and her siblings walked the two miles to the school in Sugar Hollow, which was a one-room wooden building that was later replaced with a new stone structure. Classes ranged from the first through seventh grades, and Lizzie said her favorite teacher was a young woman named Mertie Shelton, who taught "readin', writin', and 'rithmetic," along with geography and history to her pupils.

The Wyant family was active in their Christian faith and attended the Brethren Church in Sugar Hollow. Lizzie became a Christian and was baptized in the Moormon River when she was eleven. She has remained in the Brethren faith her whole life and now attends the church at Barren Ridge when she is able to go.

Always a diminutive child, Lizzie recalls that at seven or eight years old, she would ride the family horse to the gristmill owned by their cousin, John Viar, laden down with a sack of corn. John would lift Lizzie off the horse and let her watch as he ground the corn before setting her and the sack of meal back on the horse and heading them toward home. "My biggest fear was the horse would start to trot and I'd fall off," laughed Lizzie. "Why it was nothing for me at that age to walk the three miles to my grandmother's house for a visit. Nowadays you could never send a child that far by themselves for fear something would happen to them, but back then things were different. You could sleep out in the yard without fear of anyone bothering you."

As children, the Wyants had their share of daily chores, such as milking the cows, feeding the chickens and other farm stock, cooking, and helping their parents with whatever else needed to be done. But they were also allowed to play. After church on Sundays, Lizzie remembers playing such childhood games as hide-and-seek, dominoes, Old Maid, and a standard called "Annie over," which was played with a ball that was thrown over the top of a roof.

Christmas at the Wyant home was a time for excitement and happiness; the family celebrated by putting up a tree and decorating it with the children's homemade ornaments. Paper chains, strung popcorn, cut-out hearts, and sycamore balls wrapped in the foil from cigarette packs adorned the holiday tree. Lizzie said the celebration of Christmas was not limited to one particular day but an entire week, during which the family visited relatives and shared meals with them. She and her siblings set out boxes or pans that would be magically filled with nuts, oranges, candy, and perhaps a dish, mug, or some small gift on Christmas morning. It was a happy, wondrous time that Lizzie later recreated with her own family many years later.

The Wyant home was a wooden, two-story farmhouse with a living room and parent's bedroom downstairs and two large rooms upstairs where all the children slept. "The girls had one side and the boys, the other. We had trundle beds, but mostly all us kids would just sleep all together in one bed. We had wooden shingles on the roof, and one time there came a blowing snow and a fine mist was settling over the room, so Papa tacked up an old bedspread overhead so the snow wouldn't come in on us." The large kitchen was detached from the house and was later used as a blacksmith shop by Lizzie's father.

Cornelia was a loving mother who doted on her nine children, making all their clothes by hand as well as a multitude of quilts to keep the family warm during the long winter months. She had health problems and died at fifty-four years of age from complications of gall bladder surgery. Some years later, Lizzie's father married a woman by the name of Mabel Sales and had two more children by her.

The Wyant family raised all their own produce and meat, but when they needed coffee, sugar, salt, or shoes, they walked to one of the local country stores in their area; either the one run by a Harris family or Wyant's Store, which also housed the post office.

As a young girl, Lizzie was pretty and popular, and she dated five or six young men before settling on her future husband, Rubin Lester Wood, who was two years older than her. Rubin, whose fam-

ily lived three miles east of Elkton, was working in timber near
Sugar Hollow and would attend the same church as the Wyants if
the timber crew stayed over the weekend.
Rubin had dated Lizzie's older sister when
Lizzie was fourteen and still too young to
date, but a few years later when the pair
broke up, Lizzie and Rubin started to court.
Lizzie recalls a dinner on the grounds at
church that once and for all settled the question of marriage for the young couple. Rubin
was still seeing other girls at the time, and
one of Lizzie's friends asked if she thought
Rubin would take her to the dinner. "I said,
'If I'm the one he likes best, I'll be okay. But
if he decides to take someone else, then I
won't go with him anymore.' When the service was over, I left in the buggy with Rubin,
leaving all the other girls standing at the
church!"

Lizzie at seventeen

Rubin came to visit Lizzie a few days later,
asking her hand in marriage and her father's
permission to marry his daughter. On
November 29, 1923, which was Thanksgiving Day that year, Lizzie
became Mrs. Rubin Wood at a ceremony held by Preacher England
at the Methodist parsonage in White Hall, Virginia. Lizzie was seventeen, and Rubin was nineteen. Lizzie remembers wearing a blue
"trichatine" dress for her wedding, and her mother made her a
brown suit for her honeymoon. The couple did not exchange rings,
as the Brethren faith didn't believe in wearing jewelry at that time.

The newlyweds took a long honeymoon, visiting relatives along
the way before coming back to live with Lizzie's parents for a time.
"We left the parsonage and spent our first night together in my
parent's home before leaving the next day for Earlysville, where
we caught the train and rode to Broadway, down in the Shenandoah Valley. Rubin's aunt met us at the train station in a horse and
buggy, taking us to her home. That night his aunt hurried through

supper and afterward her husband, who was an Irishman, blew a whistle at the door, and all these people came to serenade us. We had such a good time and ended up staying almost a week with them before riding the train back to Waynesboro, where we spent a few days with my older sister who lived in one of the furniture company houses on Charlotte Avenue. The next night, my brother-in-law came in a Model T truck and took us back to Sugar Hollow. I remember it was so foggy going across Afton Mountain that we couldn't see the radiator, and we had to hold a lantern out the window in order to see the road. A few times, we went off the road, and the fog never cleared until we were almost to Crozet."

The first place the Woods lived after they left Lizzie's parents home in Sugar Hollow was the top floor of her sister Nettie's home in Waynesboro. Later they rented a home on Florence Avenue, then several other places in Waynesboro. Rubin found work at the Basic Witz Furniture Factory and later at Crompton's Textile Factory. He also farmed, sharecropping at different places in the area, such as the Hopeman, Wine, Dotson, and Lambert farms. Their children started coming ten months after marriage, with Wallace being born on September 21, 1924. Lizzie laughs at the memory of Wallace arriving before the doctor. Next came Lottie on December 8, 1926; Thelma on April 16, 1929; Gracie on April 13, 1931, Hiram on September 27, 1933; Curtis on June 5, 1936; Betty on January 24, 1939; Boyd on December 12, 1941; and baby Maynard on January 26, 1946.

Lizzie had several midwives, including her sister Nettie, as well as doctors Kiger and Roberts. As was the custom back then, services for a birth were paid with some type of livestock, such as chickens or a pig. Women

The Wood family before Maynard was born

had no type of pain reliever during labor and had to endure the intense discomfort without the aid of modern-day techniques. Back then there was also no such thing as baby formula, so Lizzie nursed all nine of her children. When one baby was weaned, another would soon be on the way. It was an effective birth control method by Mother Nature herself. Lizzie can still recite the amount of time between her first two children as told to her by her sister Nettie: "Two years, two months, four days, and five hours."

Lizzie washed her large family's clothes with the help of an old-fashioned washboard in a tub set on the back porch. Although she had one day of the week on which she did most of the laundry, she washed a little throughout the week so as not to have such a huge load on that one day. As one of her daughters remembers, "People didn't have as many clothes back then." It was a happy day indeed when the family finally got their first gasoline-powered Maytag washing machine.

Along with taking care of her large family, Lizzie helped her husband in the fields, working right alongside him with whatever needed to be done that day. Though she was not a big woman, Lizzie worked hard, doing a man's job along with her own and never complaining. The Wood family was a happy one, enjoying the simple things of life that fill the heart to overflowing with memories of joy down through the years.

The day that I interviewed Lizzie and her four daughters, they recalled some of these memories that are more precious than material wealth. Like the time Rubin made a wooden bobsled that could carry five people but lacked steerage. Rubin, Lizzie, and three of their children climbed aboard, thinking they could glide down the snow-covered hill by their home and maybe get enough speed to get halfway up the next hill before stopping. They underestimated their combined weight and ended up going up and down *several* hills before crashing into the outdoor toilet, spilling the entire family all over the ground! Or the times Rubin would hitch a ride to town on Saturdays, bringing home the necessary items the family needed. Upon his return, a lunch would be packed, and quilts and kids carried to the spring where a huge weeping willow tree provided shade for an outdoor picnic. "Us kids would play while Mama and Papa watched the baby," recalled Betty.

Christmas was always a memorable time at the Wood home. Gracie and her sisters recalled how they would each save a shoe-box and line them up under their parents' bed on Christmas Eve, knowing that "Santa" would fill each box with candy, oranges, nuts, raisins, socks, or clothing. The boxes were lined up in their parents' bedroom to insure that the youngsters didn't "peek" before Christmas morning.

The family picked chinquapins by the bucketfuls; Rubin spread sheets under the bushes and hit them with a stick to insure a boun-tiful harvest. They would eat some and sell some, much like the huge number of wild berries they picked during the summer months. Lizzie said it was not uncommon for her to can more than one hundred half-gallon jars of blackberries during a single summer.

Although the family did not have an abundance of money, they always had enough love and fun to go around. So much so that other relatives and neighbor kids wanted to come to their house because they knew something was always going on. They all agreed that although they worked hard, hard work never killed them.

Courtesy of Lizzie Wood

When asked what the biggest change in her life was thus far, Lizzie said that get-ting electricity and indoor plumbing had the most impact in her life. Even though having electric lights meant just a naked 25-watt light bulb hanging down from

Lizzie and Rubin in later years

a wire, she thought it was the best thing she'd ever seen. "But I think people's eyesight was better years ago than it is today," says

Lizzie. "In fact, I can still see better *without* my glasses than with them!"

Rubin passed away in 1967, and the youngest son, Maynard, bought his parent's home in Fishersville, where he and his mother continue to live. The children remain close, with most living in surrounding areas, except Wallace who lives in Maryland and Curtis who's in Washington State. Lizzie talks to most of the kids on a daily basis, and on weekends she talks to the ones living farther away. At this writing, she has eighteen grandchildren, thirty-seven great-grandchildren, eight great-great grandchildren, and is expecting two great-great-great grandchildren this spring.

Lizzie and her children in 2005

I finished up the interview by asking what an average day in the life of Lizzie Wood was like, and her answer astounded me.

I get up around something after five in the morning and see my son off to work. I fix myself a little breakfast, and after the dishes are done, I feed and water my pet parrot, Princess, and give my son's dogs fresh water. Then I take a load of laundry down to the basement and wash and dry it. After lunchtime I iron some shirts and do little chores around the house. Then I start supper, and by the time Maynard comes home and we eat and the dishes are done, there's time for some type of board game or we just sit and talk. I go to bed around ten thirty or eleven. In the springtime, we put in a big garden, and I like to work in it every day. The secret to half-runner beans is to not plant them close together. If you space them out, you'll get more beans!

I asked Lizzie if she ever took a nap in the afternoon, and she said, "No, I don't have time!"

Lizzie at her one hundredth birthday party in 2005

At one hundred years of age, Lizzie Wyant Wood is a modern-day wonder. Close to her God and her family, she continues to lead an active, vital life, offering positive encouragement to all she knows. Lizzie, for the inspiration you've given us all, may God bless you with many more years of good health and joy.

Taken from the April 2005 *Backroads*

Fresh cider being squeezed in a hand press

6

Making Apple Cider

Over the years that I published *Backroads* newspaper, the subject of sweet apple cider always accompanied the autumn issues. The first person I interviewed about cider mills was my uncle, Bill Cessna, whose father operated one in Rosemont, Ohio, early in the 1900s. He told me the basics and provided photographs showing how the process worked. In the years following, my family bought an enormous hand-cranked press to make cider out of the many apples from trees growing on our property. In October 1988, I talked to John Hailey, owner and operator of the Stuarts Draft Cider Mill in Stuarts Draft, Virginia, who was kind enough to invite me out to take photos and give detailed instructions of how apples are turned into that delicious sweet beverage we all crave in the fall months. The last mill I visited and did a story on in December 2003 was run by the Sheets family in Fort Defiance, Virginia, who were in their last year of production after seventy-three years of continuous operation by four generations. So this chapter on making apple cider is a combination of three different mills; a 1908 mill in Ohio, as well as two modern operations in our area, along with a hand-cranked variety. I found all of them to be quite interesting and their final product, delicious!

THE CESSNA CIDER MILL

When my uncle Bill came for a visit in 1986, I asked him a few questions about his father's cider mill back in Ohio, where he had been born and raised. I wasn't prepared for the amount and detail of his knowledge on the subject, and it was then that I realized that your family is a perfect source of information for preserving your own unique history.

The Cessna Mill in Ohio

Rosemont, Ohio, lies within the Mahoning Valley and is still the site of some of the most beautiful farmland this country has to offer. It is here that John E. Cessna got his start. In 1908, he made the decision to buy fourteen acres and a house with an established sawmill/cider mill business on the property. It was the same year that he married his wife, Mabel, and they began life together on the farm. John continued to operate the mill from 1908 until 1968, when he retired at eighty-nine years of age after sixty years of work.

In addition to cider, the mill was also used for making apple butter, apple jelly, vinegar, and thick-boiled cider, which was used in the preparation of mincemeat. The season ran from September 1 through Thanksgiving. After that time, it went back to being a sawmill and wood planing mill for the remaining nine months of the year.

There was no formal sign in front of the business, but folks from miles around knew it as either the Cessna or Rosemont Mill.

The Cessnas had four children, three daughters and one son, who helped with the cider-making process. My uncle's first formal job at his father's mill came when he was ten years old. He was required to "man the hopper" where the apples were dumped and make sure they were loaded properly. As he grew older, his responsibilities increased, until in the end he was cleaning the entire mill with hot, pressurized water after the last cider run was finished on Saturday evenings. He remembers the dark stains on his hands that resulted from the acid in the apples he handled.

Mill hours in the early part of the season were from eight o'clock in the morning until nine o'clock at night, Monday, Wednesday, and Friday. As the season progressed, the family worked six days a week, from eight o'clock in the morning until however long it took to get the last batch of cider run. Bill remembers his father working one day from six o'clock in the morning until one o'clock the following morning, squeezing a total of thirty-seven hundred gallons of cider; the most he ever pressed in one day.

In the early days, by eight o'clock in the morning, there would be fifteen horse-drawn wagons lined up, waiting their turn to have their homegrown apples ground and pressed into sweet cider. At that time, most farmers had some type of small orchard, and the cider was for their own family's use. The usual amount was three wooden barrels per family. One barrel was for vinegar, the other two strictly for "sippin'." I asked Uncle Bill how long the cider would keep before turning hard; he replied, "One week if it's warm . . . a little longer if it's cool." When I asked why people made so much at one time when it was just going to go bad so quickly, he just started to chuckle. I knew at once I had asked a very *dumb* question!

One bushel of apples produced about three gallons of cider, three and a half after frost. The rule was the tarter the apples, the better the cider. When he started in 1908, John Cessna charged two cents a gallon to press the cider. By 1968, the price had gone up to five cents a gallon. In 1986, I called a local mill and found the price was now twenty-two cents a gallon, and you had to provide your own containers.

If a person didn't have access to any apples of their own, Mr. Cessna would sell his cider for ten cents a gallon or eight cents a gallon if you bought the whole barrel. At that time, cider seasoned best in oak whisky barrels which were sold used for four dollars. Or you could by a new barrel for eight dollars. There were also new extract barrels you could buy from soft-drink suppliers, anywhere from a five-gallon keg to a thirty-gallon barrel that went from one to three dollars. The containers would be filled up and plugged with a wooden tap above the sediment line.

The Cessna mill was run by a wood-powered steam boiler that was kept running with the generous supply of slab wood that was sawed at the mill.

This is how the process of cider making went, from start to finish: the apples were dumped into the hopper and would travel up a conveyor to a grinder. The grinder contained a metal cylinder made up of eight razor-sharp knives that were used to chew up the fruit into tiny bits. A certain number of these bits were let down a chute onto wooden pallets. When there was about four inches built up, the pieces were then wrapped in a porous, canvas cloth and stacked fifteen bundles high before squeezing. These cloths were referred to as "cheeses." When the cheeses were ready to be squeezed, a five-foot square of metal came down from above and pressed the juice from the apple pieces. After the juice was pressed out, the dried leftovers, known as pomace, were tossed out, and the cider was filtered into a holding tank made from copper or wood. From there it was pumped through a hose into whatever container the farmer had brought.

The mill was in continuous operation because Mr. Cessna could grind one man's apples while pressing another's at the same time.

At the onset of the 1930s, beer became available more readily in stores, and cider production dropped off. Up to that time, the mill was producing upwards to 85,000 gallons per season.

Taken from the October 1986 *Backroads*

THE STUARTS DRAFT CIDER MILL

Back in the early 1930s, the Virginia Valley Orchard Company owned some fourteen hundred acres of land in Stuarts Draft and had a packing shed where workers loaded the product for shipping. Joe Hailey worked for the company and lived there in a home provided by the company. The orchard eventually went out of business in the early 1940s, and Joe purchased some of their acreage plus the old packing shed.

Today, Joe's son, John Hailey, has turned the old shed into a modern-day cider mill where folks can still purchase or press the sweet, delicious drink.

John started building the mill in 1979, and he bought the equipment he needed piece by piece, finding much of it in Arkansas, Ohio, Indiana, West Virginia, and North Carolina. He learned a lot of what he knows about pressing cider by talking to the older people and reading everything he could about it. Although the actual work on the mill began in 1979, the cider making itself started in 1984. With just John and his son working, it took two years alone to complete the huge press.

The day I came out to the mill to talk with John, I saw for myself the process that up to that point I had only written about. My uncle had done a great job explaining

John Hailey filling cider barrels

how cider was made, but it wasn't until I actually saw it with my own eyes that it all began to make sense. The process was basically the same, with the apples dumped into a hopper, ground up, and then put into "cheeses" to be squeezed. One difference in John's press, however, is that his raises *up* rather than down, so if there was ever an oil leak, it would not run into the cider and ruin the whole batch. The leftover pomace is taken by wagon out to the pasture fields and fed to the cattle. Once again, the mill is cleaned from top to bottom before the next run of cider is pressed.

Unloading apples onto the conveyor

Grinding the apples

Filling "cheeses" with the pulp

Pressing the "cheeses"
to get cider

Filling containers
with sweet cider

Removing the pomace

The Hailey press is rated at eight hundred gallons per hour in full production, and John said their best day came when fourteen hundred bushels of apples were pressed in one day. That equals about forty-two hundred gallons of cider. He says it takes six people to help with this capacity, but this is nothing for the Haileys, since John says, "In order to press economically, you have to do things in a big way."

If a person brings in his own apples to be pressed, they must have at least seventy bushels on a day that John is already pressing. On a nonscheduled day, the minimum is two hundred bushels. He does this because of the cleanup work involved. He states that it takes about forty minutes to run fifty bushels of apples; out of that, a person will get 150 gallons, since on average, each bushel will press two and a half to three and a half gallons.

John buys his own plastic containers to bottle the cider in, and the minimum order runs 360 bundles, which contain either forty-eight gallons or 108 half-gallons per bundle. This cost he passes down to the customer who is pressing at the mill. The Stuarts Draft Mill runs from October 1 through Christmas, on Wednesdays and Thursdays.

In addition to cider, John also makes old-fashioned apple butter in a copper kettle, as well as grinding corn into meal whenever he goes to an exhibit. In past years, he and his family have exhibited at the Virginia State Fair and were invited to attend the opening of the Frontier Culture Museum in Staunton. John is usually at the Fall Foliage Fair held in Waynesboro each autumn and has also demonstrated his craft at the Walton Mountain Store in Schuyler.

John Hailey slides easily into the part of an early pioneer, wearing bib overalls and talking to the curious crowds who have questions about these old-time practices. It's people like John that we have to thank for preserving the rich history of the Blue Ridge Mountains.

Taken from the October 1988 *Backroads*

THE SHEETS CIDER MILL

December 2003 marked the end of an era for the Sheets family of Fort Defiance, Virginia, as they closed the doors to their cider mill, which had been in operation since around 1930. Leon Sheets's father, Roscoe, started the business during the Depression, when all the cider mills were of the open-air variety. He found an old tire press with which to squeeze the juice from the apples and copied the machinery designs from similar mills around the area. Like the Cessna mill, people came in horse-drawn wagons and were charged two cents a gallon for the owner's service. In one season, Roscoe squeezed around three thousand gallons of the sweet beverage.

In 1960, new regulations required cider mills to be enclosed in a building, and many competitors dropped out because of the extra expense.

Roscoe retired in 1986 when he developed rheumatoid arthritis. Leon and his wife, Barbara, took over the family business, saving up vacation time from their full-time jobs to press cider during the mid-September through December season. Ten years ago the Sheets family made cider three days a week and produced around sixty thousand gallons. Today they only press half a day on Thursdays and produce eight to nine thousand gallons.

The work is hard and dirty, and the profits certainly haven't made them rich, but cider making has been a long-standing tradition in this family, and there is

Leon Sheets of Sheets Cider Mill

a certain pride in what they do. Four generations have participated in the business over the sixty years of operation.

They say one of the secrets to making good cider is to press the cider slowly. If it is pressed too fast, the cider becomes cloudy. Also, it's best to use several varieties of apples to make sure the cider won't be too sweet or too tart.

Today, the government requires all the fresh-pressed cider that you buy in stores to be pasteurized, causing the Sheets Mill to finally close their doors. Anyone who has ever sipped the sparkling taste of two-week-old homemade cider knows the new pasteurization process has taken all the zest out of the beverage.

Taken from the December 2003 *Backroads*

HAND CRANKED CIDER MILLS

In every community, if there wasn't a large mill for pressing cider, then several people who grew apples would have at their disposal a wooden mill in which to make their own cider. Our family had such a mill, and it produced many a gallon of the delicious fall beverage. Although a home mill is much smaller in size, the end product is the same, as well as the cleanup. The only problem we seemed to have while squeezing the apples into juice was that the bees liked the sweet liquid as much as we did, and it was a worrisome job trying to work around them.

A hand-cranked cider mill

The process begins by pouring the picked

apples into a hopper. A crank is turned, activating the gears below that grind up the fruit into pulp, which is put into a round wooden vat that has slats in it. Then a metal hand-cranked press is lowered down onto the fruit pulp, squeezing out the juice, which runs out into a trough at the bottom and into a waiting bucket. Before filling our plastic gallon containers, we strain the juice through a few layers of cheesecloth to remove any small pieces of apple debris. And as with all the other types of cider mills, clean-up with water is a must for the sticky residue left on everything, including your hands.

The cider can be refrigerated and consumed immediately or left out at room temperature for a few days to ferment. Making your own cider is a lot of work for a few gallons, but one taste of the fermented sparkling juice is worth all the effort that goes into it!

Della Fitzgerald at her Buena Vista home

7

Della Snead Fitzgerald

Buena Vista, Virginia

Born on a Sunday afternoon on July 28, 1907, Della was the first child of James Crist Snead and his wife, Mary Elizabeth "Betty" Fitzgerald Snead. The Sneads lived on Fork Mountain, a few miles away from the village of Montebello in Nelson County. She was the eldest of seven children born to the Snead family. A second daughter, Eva, was born in September 1908, and Della can faintly remember her as being a delicate child with blond hair and blue eyes. Eva died in 1910 at eighteen months of age. Della was not quite three at the time but remembers her daddy carrying her sister in his arms to the family graveyard to be buried. Della herself nearly died when she was nine years old, after contracting pneumonia. Dr. Drake rode his horse all the way from Fairfield to give her life-saving medicine. Della's father was determined not to lose another daughter and spoon-fed Della large amounts of eggnog until the medicine took effect. She spent nearly two months in bed before she recovered. Many said she was the sickest person they ever saw get well.

The Sneads had five more children after Eva passed away: Roy in January 1911, Ruby in October 1912, Raymond in May 1916, Vernon in June 1918, and James in January 1921.

The house on Fork Mountain where Della lived until she was twelve was a large two-story log cabin with a downstairs kitchen/dining room, living area, and a bedroom where her parents slept. The upstairs was divided into three rooms where all the children slept. It had a front and back porch and a large fireplace in the living area that had to continually be stoked with wood to heat the house. Even though her dad kept the home fires burning, Della remembers the cabin as being cold and drafty in the winter. The cabin was located by the side of the road, and it was part of an old slave farm that a man by the name of Turner, from Amherst County, bought and operated with his slaves before the Civil War. It was a large tract of land, and the virgin timber was cut and burned. The Turners raised tobacco, wheat, and corn after the war was over. The property was later cut into smaller tracts and sold to local people.

Courtesy of Della Fitzgerald

Della at age three

Della said some of the family's neighbors on Fork Mountain were the Bryants, Seamans, Fitzgeralds, and Bradleys, along with other Sneads. Walter Snead and Azella Campbell Snead, Della's grandparents on her father's side, built a house that overlooked Crabtree Falls. She always found their house to be a real curiosity, being able to watch the water plunge down over the steep rocks right from their home.

Della's father, like so many men of that era, was a farmer and did his share of logging with a team of horses. In addition to the large vegetable garden they needed for the family's food supply, they raised corn, wheat, rye, and buckwheat, which was a real treat when ground and made into pancakes. As a tribute to the mountain people's tenacity and endurance, they farmed and produced a bountiful harvest on land so rugged that valley residents would never even consider tilling it. Della laughs when she says the soil was so rocky, it was hard to find enough dirt to hill up the corn.

The Sneads also raised hogs that they butchered in the late autumn, canning the sausage meat and salting the hams and shoulders for later use. They kept milk cows, and Della says she reckons she has probably churned over a hundred and fifty gallons of butter in her lifetime. They put bells on the cows so they could tell where they were grazing on the mountainside. The family also kept chickens for meat and eggs, and they traded the eggs at the local store when they needed coffee, sugar, or salt.

There were several stores in the Montebello area back then. In the early years, one was operated by John Painter, who later sold his farm and moved west to Idaho. Albert Farris, a man from Syria, was also a storekeeper, along with one of the Seaman men. Della remembers walking to the store in Montebello with her brother to get a few groceries for their mother and carrying them the four miles home. Those were the days when coffee sold for five cents a pound. She rode in a wagon with her father to Buey Harvey's grist mill to have their wheat ground. The flour was put back into the same sacks, taken home, and emptied into large wooden barrels for storage.

The Sneads attended Mount Paran Baptist Church, riding in a horse-drawn wagon to Sunday school and the morning worship service. One of the circuit-riding preachers who pastored there was Riley Fitzgerald. Della said she wore clothing to church that her mother made, and her long, dark brown hair was either braided or worn loose with a ribbon. At twelve years of age, she became a member of the church and was baptized. They held revivals in August of each year, and those joining were baptized in the creek that ran beside Zink's Mill Road near the church.

The area children went to the one-room schoolhouse on Fork Mountain that covered grades one through seven. Della walked the mile and a half with her siblings to attend classes. One of her teachers was Effie Payne of Lovingston, who boarded with Pamphlin and Ella Bradley while she taught at the school. In the winter months when it snowed, the Snead children either stayed home, or their father would take them to school in a horse-drawn sleigh. Della enjoyed her studies, and after finishing her education, she went on to teach a few years at the same school on Fork Mountain.

When Della was seventeen, she went to Lynchburg and worked at Randolph Macon College during 1924 and 1925. She worked in the dining room and said the work was easy and enjoyable. The next year, her mother took ill, and Della did not go back to her job at the school. Her mother died in July 1926 in UVA Hospital in Charlottesville after doctors administered a blood transfusion using the wrong blood type. She was only thirty-nine years old.

Fulton and Della prior to their marriage

After her mother's death, Della stayed at the family home another eighteen months before marrying Robert Fulton Fitzgerald, a young man from Irish Creek whom she met at Mount Paran Church, where his parents, Dorsey and Eulie Fitzgerald, also attended. Fulton was a few years older than Della, but she was drawn to him, in her words, "Because he came from a good Christian family, and I thought he'd make a good husband." When asked if he did, Della smiled and emphatically said, "He sure did; in fact, one of the best." Fulton's great-grandfather and Della's great-grandmother were brother and sister.

On August 20, 1927, the young couple made the trip to the Lovingston Courthouse to be wed. Della's father drove Fulton's father's car and witnessed the ceremony along with Rev. Bob Allen, who was a distant cousin of Fulton. Once married, the couple came back to live at Fulton's home with his widowed mother for a time. Later, they rented a house close to Mount Paran Church.

Their first two children, Edgar and Edsel, were born in Montebello before the Fitzgeralds moved to Amherst, in the Buffalo Creek area, and bought a five hundred–acre tract of land on which Fulton cut timber and started his own sawmill. Della said her husband was a very industrious man and always worked hard and made them a good living. Two more children, Helen and Curtis, were born while they lived in the Amherst home. They made a final move to Willow to what they referred to as "The Whitten Place." Their last two children, Calvert and Wayne, were born at Willow.

Della says she remains a longtime Democrat, just like her father, and has voted in every election since she was old enough to do so. Her only lapse in parties was the time when her two sons, Edsel and Calvert, talked her into voting Republican when Richard Nixon was running for president. "It was the worst mistake I ever made," Della retorted strongly. "And right after that, I went back to being a Democrat!" Another good laugh the family always shared is the story of Edsel as a child coming in and announcing to his mother, "We got two good friends out there . . . God and Roosevelt!"

Della said they were all good children and learned to work early. They have all done well and have made their parents proud. Of the six, Curtis is the only child who is now deceased. He died on August 25, 1962, in an automobile accident, leaving a wife and a two-month-old

Fulton and Della on their fiftieth wedding anniversary

baby boy. Several sons have followed in their father's footsteps and have made their life's work in the sawmill and lumber business.

Della's beloved husband passed away in January 1982 after a long illness. She continued to live on at the Willow home after

Fulton and Della with family during their fiftieth anniversary celebration

Fulton's death for a total of fifty-eight years. Five years ago, she made the move to her present home in Buena Vista to be closer to her son Calvert and his wife, Mary, who live just down the street. She remains close to each of her children and has often made the cross-country trip to her daughter Helen's home in Texas. In addition to her five surviving children, Della currently has fifteen grandchildren, twenty-eight great-grandchildren, and seven great-great grandchildren.

Della finished the interview with her thoughts as to the differences in today's world as opposed to when she grew up and her thankfulness in being able to live the full life she has for ninety-six years.

"I am proud of my family. Fulton and I did our best to raise our children right, and God has been very good to me and blessed me so much. I have had it much better than my parents and the pioneer people who came to this country and settled in a wilderness. Back then, the older folks didn't have the things we do now, but they made a good living, having enough to eat and living well. Things now are so different; we have more material things and have seen more but people seem to be paying the price by being too busy and not even having time enough to know their neighbors. I have lived in a progressive age. I've seen television and radio, airplanes and numerous other modern inventions, and even watched men walk on the moon. There are parts of my life I'd like to live over again but like they always say, you can't go back."

No, Della, you can't go back but how wonderful to have memories that will last far into the future: your father and his family making mountain music, walking barefoot down a dirt road without a car in sight, listening to the whippoorwill's haunting night song and the distant tinkling of cowbells on the hillside, the laughter of all your loved ones as they share a story

Della with her son Calvert and his wife, Mary

on the front porch. You have had what we all long for . . . peace of mind, quietness of the heart, and time to savor life to its fullest.

Taken from the July 2003 *Backroads*

Vernon and Clora at their Spruce Creek home

8

Vernon and Clora Truslow

Spruce Creek, Virginia

The Truslows were one of the first couples we interviewed in the first year of *Backroads* newspaper. Someone gave us directions to their house up on Spruce Creek but didn't know if they had a telephone and said our best bet was to just drive up there to talk to them. It was a cold April day with traces of snow still on the ground when Bunny and I drove up the narrow lane up to their home, not knowing how we would be received. Bunny stayed in her Volkswagen bus while I walked with some trepidation up to the door. An older man with a weathered face, white hair, and the bluest of eyes answered my knock, and I asked if he was Mr. Truslow. Smiling, he said, "Well, I must be, because that's what they've been calling me for eighty years now." I gave the "thumbs- up" sign to Bunny, and we were both invited into the Truslow's warm and cozy home. That was in April 1982. The story ran the following month in the May 1982 issue of *Backroads*. Although it was one of our shortest interviews (we were both new to the writing business), I never forgot the heartwarming experience or Vernon and Clora in the years since. They truly were the heart of the mountain people.

Built on solid rock is a mountain home tucked away in the deep ridges of Wintergreen and bordered by Spruce Creek. In it live a warm and interesting couple who have not changed their lifestyle in some eighty years.

Making our way to the Truslow homestead seemed like an end-less task, but we bumped along the unpaved road through dense hemlock trees and partly frozen water almost to the top of the mountain. The road got so narrow that I wondered what we would do if, for some reason, we had to turn around.

The Truslow's rutted driveway was part of their front yard. Barking dogs came out from under the porch to announce our arrival. Chickens ran in all directions. One old hound dog was lazing in the sun on the front porch in front of the door. The small compact cabin sat high on a bluff. It was about eight steps up to the porch, and as we reached the top, a tall, silver-haired man in faded bib overalls greeted us with a friendly smile. Behind him was a petite woman with graying black hair who also wore a smile.

They invited us in so we stepped over the hound dog and into their home. The living room was small and furnished with simple things, but it didn't take long to spot the details that made this cabin home to the Truslows.

A small woodstove dominated one corner of the living room and had a supply of wood nearby. A brass spittoon was placed near one chair. The pictures on the wall were all family members but mostly grandchildren. A bible was lying on a table, and its worn condition indicated it had been used often. A chair in one corner held unfinished quilts, and from where I was sitting, I could see into the kitchen where a cabinet held canned goods. There were handmade bins for potatoes and onions, and I noticed that the kitchen faucet was running. I mentioned it to Mrs. Truslow, who told me with a laugh that the water came into the house by gravity, and it ran constantly. Mr. Truslow asked if we'd like to have a drink of water. I really wasn't thirsty, but to be polite we both said yes, and he brought us a glass of the cold mountain water. I remember how frosted up the glass was when he handed it to us.

Vernon and Clora Truslow, married sixty-one years, still heat their home with wood, use coal oil lamps, and make meals on a wood cook stove in the kitchen. Although they do have a gas refrigerator and a telephone, Clora prefers her wood cook stove to gas and sews on an old treadle sewing machine.

Vernon Truslow, now eighty years young, said he has lived here all of his life in this same cabin. He and one of his sons have since built a new portion onto it.

Clora lived one ridge over, on Stoney Creek, before she met Vernon. They met at school, and "it was love at first sight," she said. They courted for eighteen months and then married. They moved to this same cabin in Wintergreen and lived with his parents until they passed away. The Truslows raised their six children here, and Clora said, "It seems like we've been married all our lives. Vernon was nineteen and I was sixteen when we were wed. He worked in construction, at a lumber company, and in the apple orchards, but we have never been apart once except for him working. We've had a good life together."

Vernon and Clora on the front porch of their Spruce Creek home

The Truslows have nineteen grandchildren and twenty-three great-grandchildren. Our brief interview revealed that this was a very close-knit and loving family. Most of their relatives live nearby and all see to the needs of their parents. But it seemed that Vernon and Clora were two stout-hearted, hardworking folks who needed very little, if any, assistance as far as their lifestyle goes. Vernon still tills the rich land and grows the largest portion of their food. He also raises chickens and pigs. He had just finished planting potatoes when we arrived. He likes to whittle as a hobby but carves tool handles for all practical purposes.

I asked Clora to describe a typical day in her life. "I like to get up early; I always have and still do. I put on my coffee pot first thing 'cause we like perked coffee. Then after I wash my face and hands, I put down my bread for the day. I make enough to last us all day. Most times, I will bake a cake. I baked a fresh apple cake today. The secret to baking in a wood cook stove is to place a pan of water on the upper rack so the cake will not burn on the top before it gets done in the middle. When I finish baking, I place the bread in the upper warming ovens to stay warm and fresh all day. After I do chores around the house, I like to work at making quilts. I go to town once a week with my daughter. Vernon and I attend the Wintergreen Church of Christ."

We asked the Truslows if things have changed much in their area over the years.

"Oh well, yes, in a way," Vernon said. "People are buying up a lot of the land around here and building homes, but they are all nice people. It still looks pretty much the same here, but time has changed a few things. There used to be the old Harris Store down the way, where we could get all of our supplies, and back when I was a young boy, we all went to a one-room schoolhouse. In the winter when we had a deep snow, my father would take a cedar brush and make a path for us to walk on. When one of us got sick, we had to minister our own home remedies because there were no doctors close by, but we made out okay. For entertainment we just visited other people on the mountain or had family gatherings. Sometimes we used to 'hand fish'; that is when we'd go down to the creek and watch for the trout to go under a rock. Then we'd catch them with our hands. We'd put them in a crocus sack and carry them home to eat. Boy, they were good, too! We used to hunt all kinds of game like 'coons, squirrels, and groundhogs. They were all good eating." Clora said she liked squirrels best!

Vernon added, "There weren't too many rules back then. Now you've got to have all kinds of licenses, and it's illegal to hand fish. But our wants are few. God has been good to us, and we have many friends and have found a peaceful way of life back here. And if the good Lord is willing, we will continue that way."

Taken from the May 1982 *Backroads*

John and Charlotte Hodge; Reed's Gap, Virginia

Splitting mauls in an oak log

9

Winter Firewood

The date is December 19, 2009, and as I sit down to write this chapter, we are in the second day of one of the worst winter storms that I can remember since moving here in 1980. Back then, the weather on the mountain was colder, with a lot more snow, but in the last ten to fifteen years, our snowfalls have been minimal. It looks like that's about to change. We now have well over two feet on the ground, drifts that are over my head, and more predicted for the rest of the evening.

Outside, we may be having a blizzard, but inside, we are warm and cozy in our little cabin. That's because we heat with wood. Our stove, which is packed full with the dampers open, is a welcome respite after coming in from the barn. On either side of our Sierra stove, there is an old bentwood rocker, whose curves fit perfectly into the small of your back. We are reminiscent of Ma and Pa Kettle as we sit there drinking coffee in the mornings. Like most mountain folks, we can keep warm even if the power goes out, which most likely it will.

My first introduction to the woodstove was at Sonny and Bunny Stein's house here in Love. Our family was living in Richmond at the time, and we'd come up to visit. We noticed that their house was always toasty warm without the aid of any heat source other than wood. Up to that point, the only wood we'd burned was in the fireplace, for ambiance more than heat. Years later, our family replaced the "magic dial" on the wall with a homemade woodstove that one neighbor lady said was "ugly," but, hey, we were no longer paying a huge price for winter fuel, proving that "pretty is as pretty does!" Of course, we had to go out and get our fuel by cutting trees, but I found that I loved tromping around in the woods, gathering up the rounds of oak that my husband cut.

A respectable pile of firewood

I remember the first time I picked up an eight-pound maul and sunk it into the middle of a round of red oak; the "thunk" sound it made as the wood split in two thrilled me for some reason, and I've loved getting in winter firewood ever since. It's not for everyone and kind of pricey to get started if you've never done it before. You've got to have a wood lot, a chainsaw for cutting, a four-wheel-drive truck for hauling the wood home, and a stove to burn it in. Before you can use the wood, you've got to split it so that the pieces are easier to handle and will fit into the woodstove. And the wood has to be stacked somewhere so that it's not in your way every time you turn around. Everyone here has an ample supply, both on the ground and about a week's worth on the back porch where the weather won't get to it.

We've cut and hauled wood in the heat of August, the dead of winter, in the snow, under the light of the moon, and any other time we take a notion. It's something you have to keep on top of lest you run out when the weather is sour. With fluctuating temperatures, it's hard to know how much you'll need in any given year, so it's better to over-cut and be prepared than to under-cut and be sorry.

There are a few different ways to stack your wood for the winter. A lot of folks just put it in a big pile on the ground, and split it as they need it. If the pile gets low, you simply go out and get more. The only trouble with that is if the wood is "green" (not seasoned long enough), it's hard to start a fire with. Others prefer the circular stacking method, in which you start by leaning pieces of split wood on end against a tree or pole and continue adding layers around and on top of each other until you have a goodly pile. This is an attractive way of stacking, and you can get a lot of wood in the pile—plus it sheds rainwater very well.

My own personal favorite is ranking. Ranking means the split pieces are laid in rows, sandwiched in between two end stacks that are cross-laid for strength; this holds the rows tight and secure. I like this method because you know exactly how much wood is needed for a winter, and the rows are stacked out of your way. For instance, the year before last, we ranked five rows of firewood up

Circular stacked wood

against the side of our garage, down the fence line, and over to the barn. We used three of those ranks for the entire winter, which gave us two well-seasoned ranks to start this winter's heating, along with the two new ranks that we added earlier in the year. Of course, Billy and I differ on methods. He prefers to just dump it off the back of the truck and leave it in a big pile, while I (neat and tidy person that I am) like it ranked up and out of the middle of the driveway. We have learned to compromise. . . . He dumps it off in a pile, and once it's split, I rank it neatly against the fence.

For years, we split the wood by hand, usually with an eight-pound maul, which is great for red oak but will flat wear you out on hickory or black gum. So we progressed to a gasoline powered wood splitter, which has the ability to split just about anything growing in the woods. I could hug the person who invented the first one, and, in my opinion, it's right up there with sliced light bread. Billy lifts the big rounds onto the platform while I run the metal wedge into the center of the wood, splitting it in two. If it's a big round, we split it several times, which gives you more bang for your buck. Others continue to split by hand, if for nothing more than the satisfaction it brings.

Wood stacked in ranks

We've told you about some of the advantages of heating your home with wood, but there are a couple of disadvantages, too. There is a light film of dust that seems to cover everything when the ashes are cleaned out of the stove, which should be done each week. If there's too much ash buildup, it's hard to get more wood in for proper heating. Our stove has a built-in ash pan in the bottom that eliminates a lot of the flying dust that occurs when you empty ashes into a metal container with a shovel. However, it needs to be emptied more often. But the left-over ashes also have a productive purpose: when strewn in the soil of your garden plot, the ashes provide a wonderful source of nutrients for the earth. They can also substitute for lime, since they have twice the acid-neutralizing power of limestone. And a shovelful of ashes thrown under a tire will give it better traction in snow

The perfect winter combination, a rocking chair and a cozy fire

and ice. Place a pile of ashes in the chicken yard so that the chickens can take a dust bath. It helps prevent lice on the birds. And sprinkled inside the hen house, the ashes control odors.

In the April 2005 edition of *Backroads* newspaper, a man named Walter Mehring wrote an article about splitting mauls, and he took the photograph shown at the beginning of this chapter. Because that story was so informative, and goes with this firewood chapter, I am reprinting it for your enjoyment.

I like the "thunk!" of a splitting maul diving into wood. We called it a "Go-Devil" when I was young; an eight-pound sledge hammer, tapering on one side to a wedge. One hit usually doesn't do the trick with locust. The dense wood produces lots of BTUs and little ash, but it is hard to split. I don't try to break the dark steel free for another try. It's in there! The handle will splinter before the imbedded head pries loose. Instead, I heft a second Go-Devil and put my back and shoulders into its long, fierce arc. The "thunk" is replaced by an ear-ringing "ching!" as the partner hammer smashes against the battered sledge face of the first. A few hits like this can split about anything except black gum, big knots, and branch crotches. Some people prefer splitting wood with a sledge and a separate iron wedge. This may work as well as a pair of Go-Devils, but I'd rather avoid constantly leaning over and tapping to get the wedge started. I enjoy hearing the clashing ring of metal on metal, but these days it doesn't sound as clearly as it once did. I wish I'd been more conscientious about hearing protection in my younger days.

My two Go-Devils differ slightly in that one is made of hard cast steel, while the other is softer, more malleable iron. As a result, while the softer head has slowly flattened and spread over time, neither is likely to shoot shards of shrapnel. These days, all I see for sale are the steel variety, and they carry warning labels about the potential for bullet-like fragments from hitting two together. Truthfully, I've tried it anyway with no ill effects, though I've taken care to wear eye protection. A safer way to deal with the problem is to braze a brass surface on the sledgehammer faces. This absorbs some of the shock and makes it less likely that steel chips will fly loose. Another option is to heat a hammerhead red hot in a stove or forge, and allow slow cooling to remove its temper.

A sledge handle often breaks in a season or two because it snags spitting wood, or inexperienced helpers overshoot and hit the wood hammer handle with steel. Instead of store bought, I like to create my own tougher, rot resistant handle from a locust stave. Early in the winter, I split a three-foot, straight-grained section and leave it to dry and shrink as much as possible by the wood stove. Sledge hafting should be winter work. Handles fit in the summer shrink, loosen from their heads in the dry winter air, and your creation becomes dangerous. A draw knife easily rounds the handle into an oval shape with dimensions of about one and a half inches by one inch at the grip end, tapering to a slender seven-eighths inch neck, round in cross section, about a foot from the hammer end. I then increase the handle's diameter to a size a bit larger than the hole in the Go-Devil head, scrape the haft end of the handle down to exact size, and secure the head with a locust wedge. When in use, the taper in the handle allows flex on impact, which keeps the handle from splitting.

I've tried other woods, but locust is hard to beat. Osage orange is strong and rot resistant, but it is hard to find straight pieces, since staves tend to warp severely as they dry. Ash is less tough and rot resistant. Hickory makes a tough handle, but it rots easily.

There are often secrets within a log, which add more pleasure to the job of splitting firewood. An apparently straight-grained piece holds fast under repeated blows, opening finally to display the remains of a branch a hundred years hidden. Split red oak emits a sweet, musk-laden perfume as the rose colored wood, stained black from the impact of iron with its tannic acid, splits into thin slabs for better drying. A locust round sometimes opens to reveal a black, slow moving mass of carpenter ants, some almost an inch in length, hibernating for the winter. For the adventurous, they are edible. Seared with a little honey, their formic acid makes them taste like intense, crunchy, sweet-tart candy.

They say wood you split yourself warms you twice; once in the splitting and the other in the stove. The flex and feel of handles you've made for your splitting mauls add yet another dimension to the warmth and satisfaction your firewood gives you. Muscles and joints free up and thrill with the pleasant ache of being well used. The passion and intensity you put into an hour of steel against wood leaves you mellow and ready to sit back with friends and toast your toes with the fruits of your labors.

One Cord of Wood Contains:

    12 dining room tables

    7½ million toothpicks

    1,200 editions of *National Geographic* magazine

    942 one-pound books

    4½ million commemorative postage stamps

    30 Boston rocking chairs

Taken from the November 1982, October 1993, and April 2005 *Backroads*

Nevel and Lois Seaman celebrating their sixty–ninth wedding anniversary

10

Nevel and Lois Seaman

Montebello, Virginia

In November 1994, I was honored to attend a combination party held in honor of the Seamans' sixty-ninth wedding anniversary and their ninetieth birthdays. When the story ran in *Backroads* newspaper, both Nevel and Lois were living independently with a little help from their three daughters, Yvonne, Kathleen, and Shirley. I later interviewed them and spent a delightful afternoon talking with the couple, learning what life was like in Montebello nearly a century ago. Like so many of the other mountain people I've had the pleasure of talking with, the Seamans said growing up was a time of close interdependence on neighbors, a time of simple pleasures, and a way of life that has all but disappeared. Sit down, get comfortable, and take a trip back in time with the Seamans and relive, through their eyes, what the tiny village of Montebello was like ninety years ago.

Nevel was one of five sons and four daughters born to Elmer and Berta Seaman. The family lived in a two-story log home located just behind the present Grant's Store in Montebello. Nevel's father ran a gristmill just down the road, where the Blue Ridge Camp now stands. It was always known as the Buchanan Mill. Elmer ground the area people's corn and took one large scoop of their meal as payment for his services. If people didn't have their own corn, they could buy their cornmeal directly from him.

There was a large millpond on the property that Nevel said the children swam in during the summer months. In the winter, when the water froze, he and Lois remember ice skating on the pond. They laughed at the memory of racing up the bank to get a running start and then skidding clear to the woods on the other side with one slide.

A man by the name of Massie had sold the large, one thousand acre tract of land where they lived to several members of the Seaman family. The tract included the large log home where Nevel's family lived, which was said to have quartered slaves who ran the huge Massie farm. When the slaves were freed, Massie could no longer afford to farm the land without help, so he sold the property. Nevel said his grandfather and a great uncle came back from Philadelphia to purchase part of the property. The Seamans then broke up the land into smaller farms that they all lived on. The men who originally lived on these tracts were Modie, Dick, Willie, Jake, and Elmer Seaman, Nevel's father.

Remembering his original homeplace, Nevel said it consisted of two large rooms downstairs and two upstairs. The fireplace was so large that two armfuls of firewood could be put into it at one time. It kept the home warm during the long winter months. Although they had a kitchen with a woodstove in which to cook, sometimes they hung a big kettle of beans on an iron rod that swung into the fireplace and cooked over the open fire.

Lois remembers her mother making ashcakes, which were patted flat from cornmeal and put on the floor of the open hearth and covered with hot ashes to cook. When asked if they were "gritty," Lois laughed and said the cornmeal cakes were washed off with water before they ate them. She said she learned how to cook and do the dishes as a child of five and has been at it ever since!

Lois's homeplace was a log cabin, one and a half stories high, located on Route 686. She and her brothers, Edwin and Aubrey, were the children of Hamilton and Eliza Bradley. She recalled their home had two rooms downstairs; a kitchen and a living room that had a bed in it where her parents slept so they could tend the fire during the night. The children all slept upstairs. Lois said the house was drafty no matter how much wood they burned. When asked how cold it was, she laughed at the memory of everything in the kitchen freezing as "hard as a bull's horn." And back then, all the homes had what they called a "cat hole." This was a little opening somewhere in the wall where the cats, which kept the cabin free of mice, could come and go at will.

Lois said that nowadays mothers ask their children what they want for breakfast when they come down in the morning. Back then, a hot breakfast was already waiting on the table when the children came downstairs. Fresh pork sausage, hot bread and gravy, and all kinds of fruit were standard breakfast fare. Hen eggs were not eaten but taken to the local store and sold or traded for the things the family needed. Nevel remembers the going price for eggs back then was twelve cents a dozen.

The rugged families of the isolated Blue Ridge Mountains were totally self-sufficient. They grew all their vegetables and raised their meat products. Pork was a staple of every table, and each family raised and fattened hogs that were butchered in the fall and winter months. Beef wasn't as popular because the meat could not be cured like pork. Sometimes a small calf would be butchered and could be kept frozen in the winter.

Although canning was a popular method of food preservation, drying and burying foodstuffs was equally popular. Lois recalls her family digging large holes in the garden and lining the holes with leaves or straw and then putting potatoes, apples, or whatever they had inside the lined holes. They would lay boards on top of the holes and cover them with leaves and dirt until the fruits or vegetables were needed. She said the food would keep indefinitely and never went bad. Cabbages were turned upside down in the ground with the root sticking up. When one was needed, you simply grabbed the root and pulled it up.

They also made huge wooden barrelsful of sauerkraut and pickles; the salt brine they were pickled in kept them fresh. Apple butter was stored in large ceramic crocks in the springhouse; all you had to do was go out and dip what was needed for the day. Milk was also kept in the springhouse and if left for a few days, would turn into "clabber," which was milk that had thickened. If the clabber was put on the stove, cottage cheese could be made. The whey from the cottage cheese was given to the pigs.

Lois said that even during the Depression, they always had enough to eat. The mountain people's motto was, "If you didn't grow it, you didn't have it!" There were always three big meals a day, with fresh bread baked for each. Breakfast and dinner were the largest meals, and supper consisted of the day's leftovers.

Lois said what fascinates her most is how, with all the modern conveniences women have today, people back then had more free time to visit, read, or quilt. "We had to carry in our wood, bring buckets of water from the spring, scrub our floors with an old broom and homemade lye soap, and a hundred other chores and still had some evenings we didn't have a thing to do."

Families went to town twice a year. They'd hitch up the horses to a wagon and drive to Raphine. The horses were boarded at the livery stable while the family took the train to Staunton. Nevel remembers it being an all-day trip.

Both Nevel and Lois attended Mount Paran Baptist Church with their families. They still remember the first log church that stood a little ways down from the present church. When they attended the "new" church, it was a wooden frame building. In later years, it was veneered with bricks. Lois remembers that Paulis Massie was one of the early preachers at Mount Paran. The third Sunday in August was, and continues to be, "Homecoming Sunday," and people who have roots there still make the trip back to the church on that weekend. In years past, there was also a Brethren church located behind Homer Anderson's Store, and the Methodist South Mountain Chapel was a short distance from Montebello.

There were also many one- and two-room schoolhouses in the community. Nevel went to Peter Spring School, a two-room school located on Route 56. He said Inez Mays was one of his teachers there. Lois attended both Zink's Mill and Mill Creek schools, located on Route 686, just down the road from her home. She remembers her first teacher as being Sally Hite. Most of the teachers boarded at the home of Wade Fitzgerald. Lois said as chil-

Peter Spring School in Montebello, 1914

dren they all got a good education and that it was a much better
system than they have today. The little children started out with
a primer book with simple words and pictures. By the time they
got to the eighth grade, they had heard every lesson from grades
one through eight many times, the repetition thus instilling an
education that they never forgot.

The village of Montebello itself was a booming metropolis com-
pared to what it is today. There were people living everywhere
back then, and there were services for every need. In addition to
the churches and schools, there were four dry-goods stores where
nearly everything needed could be purchased. Besides his father's
mill, Nevel said that Beauregard Harvey also ran a gristmill. There
were also two blacksmith shops run by brothers Bob and Dan
Booth. Ed Bartley operated a barbershop on Saturdays, and you
could get a shave and a haircut for twenty-five cents. The post
office was located in the now-closed Anderson's Store.

Wade Fitzgerald, Albert Farris, Paris Robinson, and Pamphlin
Bradley were some of the first men to own vehicles in Montebello.
Wade Fitzgerald is thought to have been the very first owner, and
they called his car "Old Brasshead" for the brass ornament on the
front of the hood. Early roads were terrible in the wintertime, and
Nevel laughs at the remembrance of earning a dollar from someone

who wanted him to hook his horse up to their car, which was mired in mud.

Teenagers wishing to court usually went to the girl's home, an old-fashioned ice cream social held at one of the stores, or maybe a dance where everyone got together and listened to the music. Lois recalls going to homes where they'd push back the furniture and dance all night and half the next day. The Snead, Campbell, Fitzgerald, and Allen families would provide music for these dances, and all were fine musicians according to the Seamans.

Lois in 1922 at eighteen years of age   *Nevel in 1922 at eighteen years of age*

Nevel and Lois courted for two years before marrying. Lois remembers the first time she ever ate out, away from home. "It was at the Nelson County Fair, which Nevel had taken me to on a date. They had it set up to eat family style, with all kinds of dishes you could help yourself to." They were both twenty-one when they were wed.

The couple set up housekeeping with Nevel's parents after their December 23, 1925 wedding and continued to live there for about a year before going out on their own. They didn't start a family until two years later, when their daughter Yvonne was born. She was born at home with Adeline Allen as the midwife. Kathleen was born next with the help of midwife Alice Campbell, who ran one of the country stores. The Seaman's last child, Shirley, was born at Lois's homeplace and was delivered by Dr. Kennan. Although most of their married life was spent in the Staunton area, the Seamans eventually moved back to Montebello where they still reside.

I asked the couple what Christmas was like when they were growing up. They said the biggest pastime was visiting friends and relatives. They made music in the homes, usually with a piano or organ, and everyone joined in the singing. The children received some type of little toy, which was purchased at the country store, and a treat of raisins and oranges, which people could only get during the Christmas holidays.

"You didn't have to have an invitation to go to somebody's house back then," recalled Lois. "You just went and were always welcome. You'd hitch up the horses to the sleigh and pile the children in there, wrap them up with a quilt, and take off."

Some of the Seaman's neighbors growing up were the Ramseys, Robinsons, and the Faubers. "Ethna and Mary Fauber Seaman are just about the only girls left that I grew up with," said Lois. "The rest are all gone."

Back then, everyone got all their mail at the post office, not in individual boxes along a rural route. That convenience came at a much later date. Lois and Nevel both remember the earliest mail carrier as being a lady named Liz Carr, who lived on Irish Creek but drove a buggy to Vesuvius to pick up the mail that went to Montebello. Alec Fitch and Nelson Grant were also two early postal carriers whom they remember.

National news was slow in getting to the mountains because they were so isolated. No one owned radios or television sets, and there were only a few telephones in private homes. Newspapers could only be purchased in the bigger cities. Crystal sets, the forerunner of radio, finally made their way to Montebello, but most folks still depended on "word of mouth" to get the news of the nation and around the world.

I asked about the diseases people contracted when they were young, and Lois said there wasn't as much general sickness as there is now. When I inquired about typhoid fever being one of the biggest killers, Lois laughed out loud and said, "To tell you the truth, I think people worked so hard back then that they just plain dropped away! That, and pneumonia was the worst, I tell you. You didn't hear about folks having high blood pressure and high cholesterol and cancer as much back then. Or if they did, we didn't know what it was. We also didn't have garden pests like now, so we didn't use sprays or poisons on our crops. Why, these days you can't even grow a weed without spraying it!"

In earlier times, there were yearly cooperative traditions that people depended on to get their crops in. Lois named Rob Cash, Beard Coffey, and June Fitzgerald as three men who came in the autumn months and cradled grain for various farmers. They would cradle it and then tie the sheaths together for pickup. Lois said she could remember, as an older child, having to pick up the sheaths and put them in piles. Another job in the fall was threshing the grain. Rye, oats, and buckwheat were cut by a large threshing machine owned by the Snead family that would come to each farm. She remembers having to hold the bags onto the spout where the grain would blow out. Neighbors would follow the machine as it went from place to place until each farmer's grain was completely harvested.

Neighbors back then were more interrelated and involved with helping each other. Although they had fewer conveniences, they seemed to have a more contented life. The new people moving to the Montebello area are attracted to this characteristic and are trying to incorporate these old-time traits into their new lifestyles. It's a wonderful tradition to hang on to, and one we could all benefit from. I guess Lois Seaman summed up the whole interview by saying, "It was good living back then, and I'd love to do it all over again."

Taken from the November 1994 *Backroads*

Johnny and Nin Coffey; Love, Virginia

Veenie Fitzgerald at her Tyro home

11

Veenie Fitzgerald

Tyro, Virginia

Family and friends alike always knew her as Veenie Fitzgerald, the second child born to Mayo and Sallie Fitzgerald. Years later, Veenie's niece Geraldine Quick was looking at some early census records and noticed her name was written down as Savannah Lou Fitzgerald. How she got her nickname no one really knows, but it stuck with her throughout life.

Veenie started her life in a log cabin, along with her three sisters and six brothers. The cabin was built in Big Branch Holler, near White Rock, and was owned by her parents. Although life in general was harder when Veenie was growing up, she says it was also better.

Veenie was the eldest daughter in the family, and hard work was no stranger to her. "Why, there was none of this runnin' around like there is today. We stayed home and worked the corn or busied ourselves with other chores," reflects Veenie.

At seven years of age, she started school and walked the short distance to the one-room schoolhouse in White Rock. At that time, there were only seven grades before your education was finished. After that, the boys looked around for full-time work, and the girls made plans to marry, keep house, and prepare for raising future children.

Veenie's daddy, Mayo Fitzgerald, worked in timber, picked apples in the fall, and made wooden shingles at Mac Hewitt's barn in Love. The men all had horses to help with the farm work. Vee-nie remembers the many times that her father went to Meadow Mountain to Mont Thompson's blacksmith shop to get the horses' shoes turned, which is much like getting your tires rotated today.

Even with all the hard labor, there was also time for fun. On Saturdays, they would hike up to old Tom Coffey's ball yard and watch the boys play baseball. Veenie said she, herself, played a lot of ball with her six brothers as she was grow-ing up, and she always enjoyed watching others play, too. Some of the chil-dren would walk up to Squaremouth Rock and climb into the cave opening for a drink of the cold, clear spring water that ran through it.

Veenie (top left) with her parents and two nephews, Wayne and Lester

The mountains back then were covered with sug-arcane that people grew to have a bountiful supply of molasses. As well as the horses, oxen were sometimes used for the farm work. Vee-nie said it was her job to drive a steer that was hooked up to the cane mill to boil off molasses. "Sometimes it would take my daddy all night to boil off the cane and put it in gallon containers. [He] put up from one hundred to one hundred and fifty gallons of molasses each fall," remembers Veenie.

"And Mama made the best-tasting cakes from it during the Christmas season." Along with her mama's mouth-watering molasses cakes, there were plain scratch cakes that were eaten with no icing and multilayered apple butter cakes that were made during the holiday season. "My mother would grease up her cast-iron skillet and make a homemade batter from flour, sugar, milk, butter, and eggs. She would pour a thin layer of the batter in the skillet and cook it right in the fireplace with hot coals on top of the lid and under the pan. She'd make maybe five or six thin layers and then spread apple butter in between each layer until she had a six-layer cake."

Nowadays children go with their parents to visit people and hope that store-bought cookies will be served. Back in Veenie's day, anything store bought was a luxury no one could afford, so the children were just as delighted when some home-canned peaches were brought out or perhaps a bowl of fresh-picked blackberries with cream.

The Fitzgeralds would butcher three hogs and a cow in the fall months and salt the pork so it could cure in the hanging shed. The beef was boiled and canned for future meals. Breakfast consisted of bread and gravy with a bit of meat. They hunted rabbit and groundhog to supplement their diet, but deer and bear were not hunted the way they are now. The proverbial cornbread and beans were served nearly every day, but instead of growing tired of them, the people loved them, and that simple meal continues to be served in mountain homes even where money is plentiful for "better" fare.

Church played a big part in everyone's life back then. Veenie and her family attended the White Rock Christian Church, and she was baptized by preacher Reilly Fitzgerald in the "deep hole" just below the Massie camp on the Tye River. The old White Rock Church gradually just went downhill, and the last-known service held there was on Sunday, April 24, 1960 for Martin Fitzgerald's funeral.

Although Veenie was married briefly to Herbie Bryant, it did not work out, and she went home to live with her parents, taking back her maiden name. She had no children of her own but raised a good many of her younger brothers and sisters. Two of her brothers' wives died, and she pretty much ended up raising their children by herself. She showered them with love, and many of those children claim her as their true mother. She is also proud to say that she cared for her parents as long as they both lived.

For the last eighteen years, Veenie has made her home with Ellwood and Geraldine Quick of Tyro. Geraldine is Veenie's niece, and the love between them is quite evident as they speak to each other. Geraldine's family affectionately call her by her nickname, "Dean."

In 1976, Veenie began to be bothered by a recurring boil on her right side. She would go to the doctor, and he would give her antibiotics to clear it up, but as the months went by, the mysterious boil would reappear. She ended up going to the hospital where a doctor cleaned out the wound surgically. When the attending physician cut into the boil, he couldn't believe his eyes. Indeed, it was one for the medical books! It seemed that Veenie had gallstones that had somehow "tunneled" their way through the skin, and were lying just below the surface of the boil on her side. Dr. Penn, of Waynesboro, was stunned when he began to remove the smooth, pebblelike gallstones. Through it all, Veenie said that she had no pain, either before or after the surgery.

Two years later, again with no pain involved, Veenie began to experience a yellowish color to her skin. Cancer was suspected, and she was rushed to surgery. They found that another gallstone had worked its way into the bowel duct and was plugging it up, thus causing the yellow tint to Veenie's skin. This time, however, the offending gall bladder was taken out.

In 1981, she began to get sick to her stomach and went to see a doctor. He felt a large knot deep down inside her and suggested watching it closely. The growth began to enlarge with alarming speed, so they scheduled her for surgery. This remarkable woman once again made medical history when Dr. Penn removed a massive, twelve-pound tumor. No chemotherapy was recommended, and she was sent home. That was six years ago, and she is still going strong. I told her that I thought she was made of some "real tough stuff," and she laughed and said, "I guess so."

I loved my interview with Veenie Fitzgerald. During our conversation, I learned a lot about the early days of growing up along the North Fork of the Tye River. As long as there are older women who possess the grit and "tough stuff" that these mountains pro-

The remains of the old Mayo Fitzgerald home where Veenie was raised

duce, it will always be a source of inspiration for today's younger girls. Thanks, Veenie, for showing us how it's done.

Taken from the April 1987 *Backroads*

A healthy bunch of watercress growing in a spring branch

12

Watercress

The Peppery Perennial Loaded with Vitamins

I'm not sure where I got the idea to try to plant it, but when I moved to Love in 1980, I thought I had the perfect location to grow watercress. I think I got the seeds at the old Cohron's Hardware Store in Stuarts Draft. I brought them home and scattered them in a low spot near our spring that was perpetually wet. At any rate, the watercress thrived and continues to do so more than thirty years later.

Watercress is a cruciferous vegetable related to broccoli, cabbage, and cauliflower. Its dark green leaves are an excellent source of vitamin C, iron, and beta-carotene, which is thought to lower the risk of contracting some types of cancer. And the good news for watercress lovers . . . the green is very low in calories.

Each spring, I slip on my knee-high rubber boots and slog on down to our lower property where the watercress covers the ground like an emerald carpet. Armed with a large plastic bag and a pair of heavy-duty kitchen shears, I snip

Watercress growing in a branch of our spring

along, being careful where I put my hands lest I come in contact
with water snakes who like the bushy cover of the cress. While
stuffing my bag, I sample the goods and savor the delicious peppery
taste, which is similar to but more pungent than its cousin, dry
land cress.

A close-up of spring cress

Heather Ayers snipping fresh cress

One year I sold the cress to area fresh-produce markets and
restaurants that use it in soups and as fancy garnishes on dinner
plates. I snipped large handfuls of the cress, making sure the root
system stayed intact in the water for future picking, then wrapped
a rubber band firmly around the stems to keep the greens together.
I put the bundles in a large galvanized washtub filled with a few
inches of ice cold spring water to transport the watercress to its
destination, fresh and crisp. I charged fifty cents a bundle and was
making quite a good profit for an hour's work.

One evening, my daughter came home and found me snipping
away. When she saw what I was doing she was mortified, saying I
had stooped to migrant picking. However, when I told her I was
making somewhere in the twenty dollar an hour range, she ran
home, donned *her* rubber boots, and came back with a smile and a

pair of scissors. That spring, we both enjoyed a little profiteering. But be timely. Watercress has a very short growing season; if you don't get out there early in the season, it goes to seed and the leaves become bitter. So although it's rather short-lived, watercress is scrumptious while it lasts!

Here's a tip for planting watercress: it needs a slow-moving, spring-fed water source, away from livestock or possible sewage. A creek is not suitable because when the water rises after a heavy rain, your watercress will simply float away downstream. The root system is very shallow and delicate, and it doesn't take much to uproot it and send it on its way. The good news is that clumps of it may be pulled up, put in a container of spring water and transplanted to a new location. Just make sure that the location meets the above requirements for successful growth.

For those lucky enough to have watercress growing nearby, here are some wonderful recipes for the spring greens that are sure to please.

WATERCRESS SANDWICHES

I'm not sure where I found this recipe, but it was stuffed in my cookbook under the "wild foods" section.

6 hard boiled eggs, chopped

1 cup finely chopped chives

salt and pepper, to taste

1 cup mayonnaise

2 teaspoons white wine vinegar

2 teaspoons spicy mustard

a good handful of fresh watercress, chopped

In a bowl, gently combine the chopped eggs, chives, and salt and pepper. In a separate bowl, mix the mayonnaise, vinegar, and mustard until blended and fold into the eggs. Put in the cress and mix thoroughly before spreading on toast. Yummy!

WILTED WATERCRESS SALAD

This recipe came out of my mother's German cookbook and was originally for wilted lettuce, but I tweaked it a bit and used watercress instead.

4–6 cups loosely packed watercress

3 spring onions

4 slices bacon

1 teaspoon sugar

¼ cup vinegar

salt and pepper, to taste

Tear watercress into small pieces. Chop fine and add onions to the cress. Dice and fry the bacon until crisp. Add sugar, vinegar (dilute if too strong), and salt and pepper to the bacon and drippings. Heat. Pour heated mixture over the watercress. Toss and serve immediately. NOTE: half the bacon drippings would be sufficient for good flavor.

LYNN'S CRAWDAD AND WATERCRESS SALAD

This recipe is my own creation. I made it frequently when my daughter was young and enjoyed helping me catch the crawdads in Back Creek.

20–30 good-sized crawdads

6 cups fresh watercress, chopped (dry land cress can be substituted)

4 hard boiled eggs, chopped

½ cup chopped onion

½ cup diced green pepper

enough mayonnaise and spicy yellow mustard to hold it all together

salt and pepper, to taste

Combine all ingredients and enjoy!

WILTED WATERCRESS SALAD II

Here is another recipe I had for wilted salad that's equally delicious.

1 cup Italian dressing

2 tablespoons finely chopped onion

¼ teaspoon ground pepper

1½ quarts watercress

4 crisply cooked bacon slices, crumbled

1 cup grated Parmesan cheese

1 hard boiled egg, chopped

Combine dressing, onion, and pepper; heat. Combine watercress, bacon, and cheese. Toss with hot dressing. Top with chopped egg.

CREAMY WATERCRESS SOUP

This delicious-tasting soup can be served hot or chilled as a refreshing first course.

1 teaspoon olive oil

1 medium onion, chopped

1 pound potatoes, peeled and cut into ½-inch cubes

3 cups chicken broth

2 cups loosely packed watercress with thick stems removed

1½ cups half-and-half

½ teaspoon salt

¼ teaspoon ground black pepper

In a four-quart saucepan, heat olive oil over medium heat. Add onion and sauté until translucent (5 minutes). Add potatoes and broth, heat to boiling. Reduce heat to low, cover and simmer potatoes until tender (20 minutes).

Stir watercress into potato mixture and cook just until wilted (3 minutes). Remove from heat, stir in half-and-half, salt, and pepper until mixed. (cont. on next page)

In a blender, puree mixture, in batches, until smooth. Return soup to saucepan and heat over low heat until hot. Do not boil. Divide soup into four soup bowls and serve.

The trick to the crawdad recipe is catching the crawdads. It's pretty easy and a real blast for kids who want to help. All you need is a stick "fishing pole," a long piece of heavy string, and a small piece of raw bacon. Tie the bacon securely onto one end of the string, and tie the other end of the string to the stick. Lower the bacon into a creek that has some large rocks at the bottom and

Peyton Ayers fishing for crawdads

wait. Most times, a crawdad will come creeping out from under the rocks and grab the bacon. Don't jump the gun and pull him out too early, or he'll turn the string loose and fall off. Let him get a good grip on the bait and then lift him out and put him in an empty three-pound coffee can.

When you get enough crawdads, take them home and prepare them in the same way you would lobster: a few minutes in boiling water. The crawdads will turn bright reddish orange just like their larger cousins. Cook them no more then twelve at a time so the water temperature doesn't drop. When you take them out of the boiling water, drop them in cold water to cool the meat. Wiggle the tail back and forth, and pull it free from the body. Throw the shell away and keep the tail meat. Like shrimp, you need to devein the meat by taking a toothpick or thumbnail and running it down the center of the tail. Wash the meat in cold water and place it in the refrigerator until you're ready to use it in the salad. I guess you can cheat a little and buy crabmeat at the store, but the crawdads are more fun!

The last time I rounded up three of my granddaughters to go crawdad fishing, they were having a great time pulling them in and depositing them into a coffee can. When we had caught enough and were preparing to go back to the cabin, the youngest, Peyton, asked what we were going to do with them. When I explained the boiling process, she suddenly got a stricken look on her face but said nothing. While the other two girls and I were talking, I didn't notice Peyton pick up the coffee can and head upstream from us. I looked up just in time to see her pouring our entire morning's catch into Back Creek, saying, "I think they want to go back home to their families." We all had a good laugh over Peytie's lifesaving heroics and ended up using a substitute in our salad that day.

Portions taken from the April 1997 *Backroads*

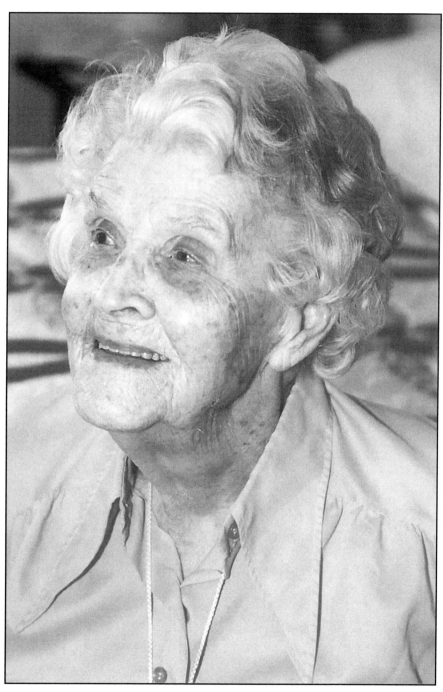

Mollie Rogers at 107 years of age

13

Mollie Wilkerson Rogers

A Woman of Three Centuries

Mollie Rogers was actually born and raised in North Carolina, but she was brought to my attention by my good friend, Ted Hughes, whose mother was living at Loyalton of Staunton, where Mollie also lived. At the time of this interview in May 2005, Mollie was 107 years old and of perfect mind. Her daughter Mary, eighty-seven, sat in with us in case her mother needed help remembering. She never had to interject and at the end of our visit, she said, "Mama had everything correct." It is truly an amazing experience to sit and talk with a woman who could tell you exactly what life was like more than a hundred years ago, and I know you'll enjoy Mollie's story as much as I did.

There aren't many people left in this world who can say they have lived during three consecutive centuries, but at 107 years of age, Mollie Rogers can not only say it but can remember it, as well.

On March 18, 1898, Mary "Mollie" Estelle Wilkerson was the third of thirteen children born to William Robert and Ara Elizabeth Brooks Wilkerson, who were married November 8, 1893. The Wilkersons had seven girls and six boys, and they lived on a four-hundred-acre farm in Olive Hill Township, near Roxboro, Person County, North Carolina.

Both of Mollie's parents were born soon after the Civil War ended; her father in 1871 and her mother in 1874. Each of her parent's mothers died when they were sixteen years old. Mollie's father, William Wilkerson, was the eldest of six children when his

mother died, and he felt responsible for his five siblings when his
father remarried. William's father eventually had eight more children by his second wife. William helped his brothers and sisters
get an education, and two
of his brothers, Charles
and Thaddeus, became
outstanding doctors in
Raleigh, North Carolina.

Mollie's parents, William Robert Wilkerson
and Elizabeth Brooks Wilkerson

One year prior to mar-
riage, William became
the overseer of a large
farm owned by Col. C. S.
Winstead, who was a
wealthy bachelor in that
area. William asked his
future bride to make out a
list of "necessities" to set up housekeeping, and at the top of the list
she had written, "washtub." Ever a practical man, William sawed
a wooden barrel in half, providing his fiancée with not one but *two*
tubs, thereby crossing off the first item on her list.

After they wed, the couple lived in a tiny log cabin to the rear
of Col. Winstead's home; it had a dirt floor, and they made do with
the little they owned. They raised a large garden, and the colonel
gave them a cow. In 1894, their first daughter, Ara Gertrude, was
born. Luckily, the cow "freshened" when a calf came along, and
they were thankful for the abundance of milk for their newborn,
since Elizabeth was having trouble nursing the infant.

Before their second child, William Earl, was born in 1896,
William had saved his money and acquired a two-hundred-acre
farm with a two-room cottage that had a detached kitchen. The
family continued to grow, having eleven more children: Mary
Estelle in 1898, Jessie Elmira in 1899, Carrie Lee in 1902, Annie
Royal in 1903, Aliene Empress in 1905, Robert Jennings in 1907,
Charles Cabines in 1909, Edgar Locust and Edna Lois in 1912,
Willard Rolland in 1915, and Thaddeus Vernon in 1917.

In 1908, Col. Winstead died, leaving money to the Wilkerson

family, which they used to enlarge their modest home to eleven rooms; it was the pride of the fast-growing family. At the Winstead estate sale, William bought an elegant three-seat carriage to replace the covered wagon in which the family rode to church on Sundays. Mollie's father continued to buy more land; by the end of World War I, William had one thousand acres. The Wilkersons were wealthy but frugal people.

Mollie remembers that the entire family worked very hard in the fields to make a living, but her kind and loving parents always made sure their children had plenty of time to play as well. Games such as jack rocks, checkers, dominoes, drop the handkerchief, andover, mumbly peg, and an assortment of card games such as Rook and Authors kept the children entertained. Mollie recalls a childhood rhyme played on the fingers that her parents recited at bedtime. It was called "William Tremble Toe," and she repeated it during the interview: "William Tremble Toe, he's a good fisherman, catches some, some none." An astonished look crossed Mollie's face as she laughed and said, "I didn't know I could still say it after so many years!"

In speaking of her early life, Mollie said she always felt loved, secure, and safe within their immediate family. She believes people were happier back then than they are today, even though they didn't have as much material wealth. Her parents, whom she called Papa and Mama, were smart, resourceful people who didn't waste anything they could put to good use, and they taught all of their children to appreciate the things they were given. They also instilled strong Christian values in each member of the family, and Mollie's faith in God has sustained her throughout the highs and lows of her life.

The one thing that was uppermost in her parents' minds was their children's education. Since the only schooling he received was derived from whatever he could learn within his own family, William Wilkerson was instrumental in starting public schooling after the Civil War in the area of North Carolina where they lived. Up to that time, there were no laws concerning schools or pupil attendance, and only a select few had the means to erect a private schoolhouse on their property to educate their own children. Students had to walk long distances to attend the elementary grades of one through seven. There was no such thing as a high school. William took it upon himself to donate timber and a parcel of land at the edge of his farm for a public school that would have grades eight through ten in addition to the elementary grades. He and his neighbors then built the structure, and William offered to let the teachers board with his family, giving his children the extra benefit of educational influence in their home.

Jamie Rogers's parents had privately educated their son until he enrolled in the high school located on the Wilkerson farm for the 1911–1912 school years. The Rogerses had moved to the area when Jamie was fifteen, and he and thirteen-year-old Mollie had immediately fallen in love. She remembers him writing a love note and placing it on her desk. After reading the note, Mollie took it home and showed it to her sister Gertrude, who kept her secret. Jamie gave Mollie a box of chocolates on her fourteenth birthday and, later, a pearl lavaliere to wear around her neck, but Mollie was afraid to show it to her mama

Mollie at age fourteen and Jamie at sixteen in July 1912

for fear she'd tell her daughter she was too young to accept such a gift. But she needn't have worried because her family thought as much of young Jamie Rogers as Mollie did.

In the fall of 1912, Jamie left for Warrenton, and the two young people wrote letters to each other in between the times he came home for visits. Before she was fifteen years old, Jamie gave his future bride a beautiful gold bracelet with her initials on one side and engraved flowers on the other; she still wears it today. She accepted this gift openly, and the couple began their formal courtship at this time.

Mollie was an excellent student and received a full scholarship to Elon College after graduating from high school. She remembers that at seventeen years of age, she went in a horse and buggy to the Roxboro depot, where she boarded the train and rode in a Pullman car to college. During 1914 and 1915, Mollie was a student at Elon, and during the 1915 to 1916 term, she attended North Carolina College for Women, which is now the University of

Seventeen-year-old Mollie in 1915

North Carolina in Greensboro. She completed two years of college and received her teaching degree. She moved in with her older sister Gertrude to fill her first teaching position in a one-room schoolhouse located near her sister's home. Mollie taught for only one year before marrying her childhood sweetheart, James Henry Rogers, on August 7, 1917; she was nineteen. James, whom she always called Jamie, had just completed four years of college at North Carolina State, with a degree in agriculture.

When asked about their wedding, Mollie said that she and Jamie were married in the parlor of her parents' home; she wore a new navy-blue serge suit with a white blouse, black shoes, and a navy-blue hat. With her glossy black hair, everyone commented on what a beautiful bride Mollie made. The newlyweds left on that day's train for a week-long honeymoon trip to Hickory, North Carolina. When they returned, they began farming land that adjoined the Wilkerson farm that had belonged to Jamie's father and grandfather Rogers. Three of Mollie's seven children were born on the farm: Mary in 1918, James in 1919, and Emma Jane in 1923.

On the farm, they grew corn and wheat for animal feed and maintained a huge vegetable garden for their family's food supply. Mild

temperatures and a longer growing season in North Carolina
insured a healthy diet throughout the year. Although the cash crop
at that time was tobacco, Jamie was against smoking and thought
farmers of that era should diversify, so he borrowed money to start
a purebred livestock farm. They were doing well until a recession in
1922, and the bank called their loan. The couple lost everything
they had worked for
but managed to sell
their farm to Mollie's
father. For the next
three years, they rented
a place belonging to
their grandmother.

In 1925, a relative
died and left Jamie an
inheritance that pro-
vided a nest egg for
the family. A few
years later, they saw a
Virginia farm adver-
tised in the newspaper

Mollie with her first two children, James and Mary

and began to make
inquiries about it through the mail. In February 1927, the Rogerses
moved to Bedford County, Virginia, to a sixty-five-acre apple
orchard with a mountain home near the Peaks of Otter, close to
Terrapin Mountain.

They worked the orchard, and Mollie vividly remembers how
the apples were neatly packed in a circular tray that sat atop the
other apples inside a wooden barrel. These barrels were then
trucked to the train station at Big Island and moved to Roanoke
for storage before being shipped to England. In a few years, they
were able to buy a second orchard in Big Island, Virginia. By this
time, four more children had been born: Rebecca, Patricia, Nancy,
and Walter.

Jamie began working for the Roosevelt Administration. He
worked first in the Rural Rehabilitation Administration, helping

farmers to get government loans to keep their farms, and later for the R.E.A., where he worked tirelessly to get electricity in the rural areas of Virginia. Since 1918, Jamie had been interested in bringing electricity to the country people, and he installed a Delco generating plant on their property; soon other neighbors followed suit.

The drought of 1930 and the Great Depression years brought hard luck to everyone, including the Rogers family, but with hard work, the family began to bounce back. In September 1942, Jamie went to Baltimore, Maryland, to train to be a supervisor in the parts division of the Glenn L. Martin Airplane Factory in the Middle River suburb of Baltimore. They saved enough money to put all five daughters through college. After World War II ended, Jamie did not get laid off as expected but continued to work at the Martin Factory.

By 1961, their last child, Walter, was in college, and Jamie and Mollie retired to a beautiful farm that they had bought ten years earlier. It was called Beechwood and was located in rural Louisa County. Later, they designated one square mile of the farm to Virginia Electric and Power Company for the development of Lake Anna. Mollie remembers thinking she would miss seeing the cattle grazing on the expanse of pastureland once the property was flooded, but after the lake was established, she could sit on the porch and watch geese swimming on the glistening water, which she said was just as pretty a picture.

Mollie and Jamie at ages eighty-eight and ninety, respectively

Jamie and Mollie continued to live at Beechwood which, by this time, had become a valuable piece of lakeside property. Jamie passed away in 1991, and Mollie stayed at the farm until November 1992. Then she moved to Fort Defiance to live with her daughter Mary and Mary's husband, Fritz Stout.

Mollie became a resident at Loyalton of Staunton four years ago and continues to enjoy the family and friends who come to visit. The assisted-living facility held a birthday party in March to celebrate Mollie's 108th birthday, and it is clear that she is a very important and well-respected member of the Loyalton family.

Looking back through the 108 years of Mollie's rich life, I asked what she thought the greatest change has been. I was not surprised to hear that she thought it was the breakdown of the American family. Quoting an early journal she wrote called "Mollie's Musings," she gave her view on family.

"I think the reason we have seen our moral values change so much is due to the parents wanting to give their children a better life than they had. As each one of us starts competing for a share

Mollie at 108 years old

of the 'good life,' we don't see or smell the roses along the way. I read that one man said much of the drug use and crime in today's world is due to parents not having time for their children. Children need the love and security of a close family life but don't always have it since mothers and fathers alike have to work in this atomic age."

These are very wise words from a wise woman. Thank you, Mollie Rogers, for being an excellent role model for everyone you've come in contact with throughout your life. May each of us strive to live godly lives like your own so that future generations will know, and pass on, the unique bond of close and loving families.

Taken from the May 2005 *Backroads*

Gordon Patterson in front of the old Lyndhurst train depot

14

Charles Gordon Patterson

Sherando, Virginia

Charles Gordon Patterson is the chief patriarch, historian, storyteller, and much-respected native son of the little village of Sherando. Of all the people I've met since moving to Virginia, Gordon is the one man who no one has anything bad to say about. Everyone adores him, especially his grandkids.

Gordon spent the first twenty-nine years of his working life as a telegraph operator for the Norfolk and Western Railroad. The other twenty-four he served as postmaster for the Lyndhurst Post Office. He also had a brief stint as a coal miner. It was my privilege to talk to Gordon about his early years, and in doing so I received a wealth of information about his professions and the area in which I live.

Around 1935, Gordon started his apprenticeship as a Norfolk and Western telegraph operator at the Lyndhurst railroad depot. He walked the five miles from his Sherando home to the depot twice daily for a year while learning his trade. Telegraph training is a slow process. The ear is not naturally attuned to the clicking sound of Morse code, so it takes a long time to be able to send and receive messages with any speed. One who is proficient at it should be able to send messages as fast as one can type on a typewriter. Gordon laughed as he told me he used the "biblical system" of typing called the "seek and ye shall find" method!

When there were no messages being sent, he helped the postmaster, Albert Finter, with duties in the post office, which was

Gordon as a boy

*Gordon in West Virginia
when he was a coal miner*

located inside the train depot. A year later, Gordon held rights as a telegraph operator from Winston-Salem, North Carolina, to Hagerstown, Maryland, on the Shenandoah Division.

The different shifts were called "tricks." Gordon said they consisted of three shifts from 8:00 a.m. to 4:00 p.m., 4:00 p.m. to 12:00 a.m., and 12:00 a.m. to 8:00 a.m. Gordon worked forty-one stations on the Valley line of the railroad and eight places on the Western line. He recalled, "You'd have to work as many days at each station as they'd want you to. You would ride the train to your destination, and the company would pay you time and a half for travel. We had codes we used over the wire that we understood, such as 'twenty-five on the wire' meant 'I'm busy . . . call me back later.' 'HR' meant 'hands ready' (I'm ready to receive a message). And '2-copy' always meant to make two copies of the letter."

Gordon married his wife Katherine on July 11, 1941, in Norton, Virginia. The first place the couple set up housekeeping was in Walnut Cove, North Carolina, where Gordon was working at the time. The Pattersons moved around quite a bit but finally came back and settled in Sherando, where they were both from originally.

Gordon said, "I tell you the truth, when I reminisce and think about the good times I had on the railroad, I realize that it gets in your blood and never quite goes away. We have a group called the Shenandoah Valley Retired Railroaders Association that meets twice a year for a meal and general get-together, and we always have a good time."

Gordon (far left) with his brothers, Allen, Stanley, and Maynard, in 1940

Because of all his early training in the post office, Gordon decided to resign from the railroad when a job as postmaster came open. On January 19, 1951, he became acting postmaster of the Lyndhurst Post Office; on June 30, 1952, he was appointed to the office. Along with his new title, he continued to act as telegraph operator, express agent, and freight agent all rolled into one. The Western Union was also located in the train depot, and one of Gordon's saddest duties was to hand-deliver casualty telegrams to the families of men who had lost their lives in the Korean War. He said that the government would authorize and pay for a taxi for as much as five dollars if the family was outside walking distance. Gordon remembers another sad incident when a man by the name of Levi Yoder was killed while he was walking across the railroad tracks and failed to see an oncoming train.

As postmaster, Gordon had to sort the mail and put it in people's boxes. The mail for people who didn't have a box at the post office, he would place on the carrier's desk, and the route carrier would sort it according to the boxes along his route. Although Andy Allen was the rural mailman when Gordon had started, it was Reginald Hatter who carried the mail once Gordon became postmaster. Gordon's finest compliment came from Reginald, who said, "It didn't make any difference to Gordon Patterson who came in the post office. If a person was a millionaire or a hobo, he treated them all the same." People responded in kind, bringing Gordon all sorts of gifts and coming in just to visit and talk with him. Gordon remembers with fondness two of his favorite black men, Walker Burden and John Vest.

"Walker had post office box number twenty-three, and he was just such a nice fella to talk to. John would come and walk down the tracks in the spring and pick creasy greens. He'd come in with a big bag of them for me, and I'd offer to pay him, and he'd always tell me, 'Why you don't owe me anything, Mr. Gordon, but maybe I'll get you to help me fill out my tax papers when they come.' And I would, too!"

Gordon recalls that Tazewell Tench always had post office box number eleven from the time he moved to Lyndhurst until he moved away. "When we moved to the new post office in 1969, I saved box number eleven for him over there, too."

Lyndhurst in the early days was nothing but rural farmland, with houses few and far between. In the 1930s, when Gordon was still making his daily walk to the station, he said it was not uncommon to walk there and back without seeing one vehicle on the road. He said that Lyndhurst was classed as a "star route," which meant individual contractors could make a bid on it if they wanted to carry mail for that area. The lowest bid always got the route.

The carrier after Reginald Hatter was Robert Monroe. After him, the route was consolidated with Stuarts Draft's, and Homer Hinkle carried both routes. Years ago, a postmaster got paid by how many stamps he cancelled in one day. The newspaper printed a list of unclaimed letters at the end of the month. If no one came to claim them, they were sent to the dead-letter office in Washington, DC, which would try to return them to the sender.

Gordon recalled, "Some of my fondest memories were of the school children who used to come in the depot while waiting for the bus. I used to jaw at them about everything, and if one morning I was kind of quiet, they'd whisper to each other, 'You better be quiet . . . Pat's a griping!' For the ones afraid to cross the tracks alone, I went out and walked them across."

Postal hours back then were Monday through Saturday from

eight in the morning until five in the afternoon, but many days Gordon would go in at six o'clock in the morning. The office was partitioned from the railway station with wooden pigeon holes for the mail slots. For heat there was a woodstove.

Marian Davis, Gordon's successor, remembers being his part-time clerk from 1952 until 1969. She said the worst part of work-ing at the old depot was the "Johnny house" out back, which she just *knew* was filled with snakes. She opted to walk over to neigh-bor Christine Floyd's house to use her bathroom when the need arose.

Gordon at Mount Torry Furnace in Sherando, 1981

In February 1969, a new mod-ern post office was built just up the road, and they all moved into their new quarters. Gordon con-tinued to serve at his post until his retirement in 1976, at sixty-five years of age. Marian Davis suc-ceeded him as the new postmaster until March 1, 1984. In August of that year, Bruce Chandler was appointed.

Many changes have occurred since the early days when Gordon Patterson became postmaster. It seems that paperwork has replaced people, and stress is an on-the-job given. Gone are the days when ruffled curtains draped the front window, and punch and cookies were served in the lobby on Valentine's Day . . . and a man by the name of Charles Gordon Patterson had the time to hold a small hand and walk a frightened child across the railroad tracks.

Taken from the October 1994 *Backroads*

The men of Camp 8; Sherando, Virginia

15

Civilian Conservation Corps

The 351st CCC, Camp 8; Sherando, Virginia

My first solo edition of *Backroads* newspaper was February 1983, Volume 3, Number 15. I promised God that if there was a good front cover story for that month, I would continue to publish the paper by myself. Enter Dave Benavitch, a U. S. Forest Service employee who came to my cabin door with material and photographs of Camp 8, the CCC Camp located about five miles down the road at Sherando. Because of him, I decided to continue to do *Backroads*, although I was scared out of my wits. This is the article I wrote.

The year 1983 marks the fiftieth anniversary of the construction of the CCC Camp, located at Sand Spring, a little south of Sherando. The initials stand for Civilian Conservation Corps, an organization begun by President Franklin D. Roosevelt in an effort to curb unemployment during the Great Depression of the 1930s. The chapter picture shows several area men who were stationed at Camp 8, one of five such camps in the Pedlar District.

The 351st Company was organized at Fort Monroe on May 8, 1933. In the same month, 185 enrollees, four officers, and four regular army enlisted men left Fort Monroe for Sand Spring, Virginia.

Eleven days later, they arrived and set up camp. The first rule of order was to clear the land for future buildings. They removed rocks, cut trees, and hauled water from nearby Sand Spring for cooking and drinking. The men washed themselves and their clothes in the crystal waters of Back Creek, which still winds peacefully down the same mountain hollow today. The men, despite their primitive surroundings, went to work with a true pioneer spirit and built a camp that was later considered the best looking in the state.

By the summer of 1933, a mess hall, complete with electric lighting and indoor plumbing, was constructed. That same

The barracks at Camp 8

The Camp 8 chapel

autumn, new barracks and a recreation hall were finished, and the grateful men took down their tents and moved inside for the winter. The recreation hall became the main attraction for camp members. Bone-weary men looked forward to the various activities held there after a long day of working in the field. Movies were shown, plays and skits were put on, educational classes were available, and parties were held for the CCC workers. Morale ran high at the recreation hall.

The camp was located at a point near the northeastern end of the George Washington National Forest, with the goals of timber stand improvement and forestry work. The first step in this direction, and to facilitate fire control, was the construction of fire trails and forest roads to give easy access to the growing timber. Later, the construction of a lake/recreation area (Sherando Lake) and a planned game refuge (Big Levels) were incorporated into the work program.

Big Levels Game Management Area came about largely through the efforts of Mr. Justus Cline of Stuarts Draft and Judge A. Willis Robertson of Lexington, Virginia. Both men were closely associated with the Sherando Lake Recreational Area project.

The actual lakebed clearing started in February 1934. This, along with the work of cutting down trees, started the biggest single project of the United States Forest Service in Region 7. By the time the project ended, these once relatively unskilled men were experts in stone masonry, carpentry, landscaping, concrete construction, and plumbing. They acquired their new skills through actual work on the project under the instruction of the technical service.

Camp 8 was directly responsible for building and maintaining several area roads and also for the construction of six local mountain trails in addition to part of the Appalachian Trail that runs through this district. Records confirm that the Appalachian Trail was once an ancient Indian footpath which ran along the crest of the Blue Ridge Mountains. The CCC members elaborated on and rerouted much of the trail, and many an avid hiker today has the Civilian Conservation Corps to thank for the breathtaking views they are privileged to see along the way.

CCC men constructing the Blue Ridge Parkway near Love, Virginia

The entrance to Camp 8 on the desolate main road to Sherando

The CCC boys were also responsible for the construction of the Coal Road, which runs fourteen miles from Back Creek in Sherando to the Saint Mary's River; Campbell's Mountain Road, which runs from Love to the Tye River in Nelson County at Route 56 in Tyro; and the Sherando Lake road, which is two miles from Back Creek into the lake itself. Camp 8 also maintained the

Howardsville Turnpike from Sherando to the Blue Ridge Parkway, along with the various telephone lines strung along the roads.

Trail construction in the area included Torrey Ridge Trail, Turkey Pen Ridge Trail, Kennedy Ridge Trail, Stoney Run Trail, Bald Mountain Trail, and Cellar Mountain Trail. Anyone who has driven down these trails can appreciate the hard work that went into making them.

Camp life enriched many of the local men's lives during the Depression. One man was quoted as saying, "We ate better on one regular workday than we ever did on the best of Christmases back home." Lean frames filled out under the careful nurturing of camp cooks such as Alton ("Fats") Lewis. Although the men were required to live at the camp while they held their government jobs, those lifesaving paychecks made sure the ones at home weren't going hungry, either. Many area men said they would have probably starved to death if it weren't for President Roosevelt's "Make-A-Job" program.

Along with all the hard work the men did during that time, there were some sideline activities that amused everyone. Camp 8 adopted two baby black bears, and they became very tame as the men bottle-fed them and showered them with attention. Another big hit was the camp newspaper called the *Spring Owl*. This was a weekly publication, and the first time I was privileged to read it, I was highly amused at some of the clever wit and humorous innuendos the men used when writing the paper. They were careful never to tell the whole story but kept you guessing as to "who done what."

Not only did the CCC Camp house government workers during the Depression, but it also became a local POW camp when World War II broke out. About 150 German prisoners were housed in the barracks, and many participated in painting "stained-glass" pictures on the windows in the chapel. These beautiful windows can be seen today in the history room of the Waynesboro Public Library. Two German prisoners by the names of Hans Schages and Karl Baumann, who were interred at the detention camp in Sherando, received such good treatment by the Americans that although both returned to Germany after the war and married, they came back to become citizens in a land that was no longer foreign to them.

I interviewed Karl Baumann and asked him why he had moved to the U.S. Karl said that after the war was over, he had stayed on at Camp 8 for a time and hired himself out as a laborer to the Galen Heatwole farm near Stuarts Draft. He said that Galen, too, had shown him great kindness, and he recalled an incident that permanently swayed his opinion of the American people.

"I remember the first day I went to work. I was so hungry that I took a cob of corn from the corn crib and was eating it when [Galen] saw me. He asked what I was eating, and when I showed him, he said that corn was for chickens. Then he disappeared into the house, and when he returned, he handed me a big glass of milk and some fresh sandwiches. It tasted like a banquet! I thought about the verse in the Bible that says, 'If your enemy is hungry, feed him.' Because of Galen and his family's kindness to me, I decided to move to America . . . where people treat you fairly."

Portions taken from the February and March 1983 *Backroads*

Lottie Corbett; Waynesboro, Virginia

Lillie Napier at her home in Nellysford

16

Lillie Pearl Puckett Napier

Nellysford, Virginia

September 29, 2003, marks the ninety-fourth year that Lillie Pearl Napier has spent living near the quaint village of Nellysford.

Lillie grew up on Old Stoney Creek and was the firstborn daughter of Luther Lynnwood and Nannie Beatrice Thompson Puckett, who lived on the twenty-acre homeplace. Lillie had two brothers and two sisters: Chesley, Arthur, Irene, and Hilda. Lillie said that as children they worked hard but were loved by their parents and had a good life up on the Creek. "Mama and Daddy were good parents who didn't whip us all the time . . . just when we needed it. Sometimes Mama would smack me on the shoulder for picking a fight with Irene. When that would happen, I'd tell Irene that she was Mama's 'pick.'"

Luther Puckett, son of Molly and Bob Puckett, worked at a sawmill, did some logging, farmed the land, and, like so many others at that time, picked apples during the fall months. Nannie, daughter of Cornelius and Catherine Thompson, stayed home to raise her children and tend the heavy workload of a mother of that era.

The Puckett children were expected to help with everyday chores, such as cutting weeds in the garden, milking the cows, sweeping the yard, carrying water from the spring, washing and ironing clothes, as well as a host of other jobs that had to be done for the family to survive.

The two-story homeplace had four rooms downstairs and two large rooms upstairs. As a child, Lillie loved sleeping in the upstairs bedroom, especially when it rained, because the sound of rain hitting the metal roof was soothing. "When it rained hard, you could actually hear the rocks rolling down the creek. After I got married, if a rainy night came and I had a hard time falling to sleep, I'd call Mama and say I was coming back home so I could get a good night's sleep!"

The Puckett family raised a big garden and put up food for the winter by drying, burying, and canning, which was done outside in large metal tubs over an open fire. They kept cows for milk, butter, and other by-products that the large family consumed. Lillie can remember the sound of cow bells ringing through the hills, letting her folks know the location of each animal as it grazed. Hog meat was an important staple, and the Pucketts raised several spring pigs to butcher later in the fall, close to Thanksgiving. Hams, shoulders, and side meat were smoked, and sausage was made and canned for later use. Nearly everyone kept chickens, so eggs would be readily available for the large breakfasts that were served at that time.

Lillie and her siblings walked to school in Nellysford, which was about two and a half miles away from her home. She remembers an older black couple who lived along the way and how she and her siblings would carry wood up onto the porch for them. "We called the man Uncle Sam, and one day I remember his wife was roasting chicken on the open hearth to take to the Small family who had sickness. Those chickens smelled so good that I told my sisters I thought I would just stay there and help instead of going to school. It took a lot of talking on everyone's part to get me to leave that day," laughed Lillie. The school at Nellysford had classes up to the seventh grade, but Lillie, as the eldest child, was needed at home and did not complete her studies.

Her best friends when she was a child, and throughout life, were Trosey Allen, Louise Truslow, Thelma McGann, and Robie Campbell. They walked to each other's houses to visit and sometimes to play hide-and-seek or tag. Back then, children would gather at the "buck hole," a deep spot in the river where they could swim.

Washday at the household was a big chore that required carrying water from the spring to boil outside on an open fire. The clothes would then be boiled in a large kettle and scrubbed on a washboard, rinsed, squeezed, and hung out to dry. Lillie remembers getting a good start on the ironing the same day the clothes were washed and finishing up the next day. Several flatirons were kept warm on the wood cook stove to accomplish this never-ending task.

Christmas at the Puckett home was one big get-together. Lillie recalls that everyone up and down Stoney Creek would visit. "We'd go from house to house, playing games, making candy, sharing a meal. Our family had a live tree which we would decorate. Mama left us kids at Granny's house while she went Christmas shopping in Nellysford. She told me not to peek inside the bags she brought home, but I did and found two doll babies, one dressed in pink and the other in blue. I liked the one in pink. On Christmas Eve I told Mama, as I was going upstairs to bed, that I hoped Santa Claus would bring me the dolly in the pink dress. She knew at once I had peeked at the presents and told me she wasn't going to give me the doll at all but Daddy made her, and she told me I was Daddy's pet, which I guess I was since I helped him do everything on the farm."

One of Lillie's first jobs as a young girl was picking apples at Mr. Buck Rodes's orchard in Beech Grove. "The first year I worked, I made two dollars a day, which was pretty good money back then. Someone would pick us all up in a big truck, and we'd ride over to the orchard and pick all day. I loved picking apples, especially climbing the ladder. I'd climb off the ladder into the tree itself and hang my basket out on a limb. I'd fill it so full that someone would have to help me lift it from the branch and lower it to the ground. Men in trucks would load the apples and take them to the packing shed where they were put into wooden barrels and taken to the train depot in Afton; [from there] they would be shipped to different parts of the country."

When asked who the doctor was in the Nellysford area, Lillie said Dr. Everett used to ride on horseback to make house calls. In later years, he drove a vehicle. The two midwives, who attended home births, were Nellie Cook and Mrs. Miller. All of Lillie's children were born at home except her last, who was born in Charlottesville.

Lillie married Cashus Napier when she was twenty years old and he was thirty-six. They met at Wintergreen Christian Church and courted for a few years before marriage. Courting back then consisted of Cashus walking up Old Stoney Creek to visit and talk with Lillie in the evenings. When asked how long he'd stay, she said her father would drop a shoe on the floor from his upstairs bedroom as a signal for the young man to take his leave. The Napier family lived one ridge over on Spruce Creek, and Cashus would walk the fields between their homes when they began to court. There were fifteen children in his family, and Cashus was one of twins, whom the doctor dubbed Sir Cashus and La Dishus Napier. Lillie called him "Cash" and laughed at the names he and his brother were given, saying, "Names must have been scarce back then. Either that, or the names Dick and Harry were all used up. I'd call him 'grandpa' just to try and get a rise out of him, but he'd just laugh, and I'd end up being the one mad!"

The couple married on December 26, 1929, in Wintergreen Church, leaving on a week-long honeymoon from the Afton train depot and riding to Washington, DC, where Cash's three sisters lived. Lillie remembers going every day to see all the sights and visiting all Cash's relatives in the evening. After returning, the couple lived with the Napiers for a few months before moving to the 250-acre farm they bought closer to Nellysford. The four-room home on the property belonged to Lillie's aunt, Betty Fitzgerald, who had since moved to Stoney Creek.

Lillie recalled an incident that happened there before she and Cash were married. She and her girlfriend, Orie Whitlock, were out gathering creasy salad one day and stopped at the old home, which was then vacant. They found some old clothes upstairs and went to work dressing up two poles they nailed together, setting up the scarecrow in front of the window. Later in the day, Cash and his brother had come to work in the fields; Cash saw the bait and knew who had set it. He sent his brother upstairs on a makeshift errand and laughed as he came flying out of the house, exclaiming, "There's somebody dead up there!" When asked about it later, Lillie confessed to the bit of mischief.

Back then, the land was mostly fields, which the Napiers farmed. Cash timbered the mountain land that lay to the west of them. The couple raised most everything they needed to survive and walked down to Forest Hughes's store in Nellysford to buy coffee, sugar, salt fish, and other staples. When they needed cornmeal, Cash would load up a large bag of dried corn onto his horse Blaze and ride down to Grover Harris's mill where it would be ground into meal. The miller would take a portion of the meal as payment for his services. Blaze had a colt by the name of Teeny that would always tag along on the trip to the mill.

Lillie worked alongside her husband on the farm, planting crops and tending them. They had a team of horses and the standard farm animals, such as milk cows, hogs, and chickens. Lillie churned cream in a wooden churn and packed the sweet yellow butter in a round mold that had a double wheat pattern on the inside. She cooked on a Home Comfort wood cook stove and loved frying up potatoes in the rich butter she had churned with her own hands.

Lillie and Cash started their family on April 23, 1931, when their first and only daughter, Audrey, was born. Two years later on April 27, Franklin, the first of their four boys, came along. Next in order of birth came Roy on July 3, 1935; Norman on June 14, 1939; and the youngest, Massie, on February 27, 1942.

The Napier children started out walking to the same school in Nellysford that their parents had attended. By 1939, however, busses had begun to pick up the children and take them to the new Rockfish School. But they still had to walk the mile and two-tenths out to the main road to catch the bus. Like their parents before them, all five were expected to help with the farm chores.

Frank, who was there with his wife, Pat, and niece Cindy Baker the day I interviewed his mother, remembered how they harvested the many vegetables from the fields, drying, canning, or burying them for later use. He said that they kept apples in a wooden trough lined with hay inside the barn, and the onions were hung in the corn crib where they never rotted before they were used. The potatoes and turnips were buried under the ground and dug up when needed.

Lillie made use of the food they raised, staying in the kitchen a good bit of the time,

An early Napier family photo: (back row, L–R) Norman, Massie, Frank, and Roy; (front row) Cash, Lillie, and Audrey

cooking for her family. She said that she made three hot meals each day, and fresh bread was served at each meal. Usually hoe-cakes or biscuits for breakfast and dinner and cornbread with supper. Breakfast consisted of ham or bacon, plenty of fresh eggs, gravy, and bread. Lillie laughed and said she'd no sooner get breakfast over with and dishes done before it was time to start the whole process over again. "I'd stay in the house, cooking all day."

Cash did a lot of hunting that supplemented the family's diet with venison, squirrel, turkey, and trout. The smokehouse was always full of hams, shoulders, side meat, and bacon—all of which were smoked with hickory wood. Frank remembers the wonderful aroma when the meat began to drip in the fire and how his father's clothes would carry the smell of hickory smoke for days after the task began. He remembers how delicious fried country ham and red-eye gravy was.

The family picked gallons of blackberries and huckleberries in season, which Lillie would then can or make fresh pies and jellies with. They would get up early and go pick at "Graveyard Hill," where the early people such as the Colemans were buried. They cut creasy salad, which grew thick in the fields, and Lillie would boil it until tender, then add some fat meat and grease to it for supper. They would gather black walnuts and make money by selling them, or crack them for the nutmeats that Lillie would use to make

Lillie with her son Frank; granddaughter
Cindy Baker; and Frank's wife, Pat

her delicious black walnut fudge.

Cashus Napier died in 1981 at eighty-seven years of age. When asked if he had been a good husband, Lillie was quick to reply. "Indeed he was, and if he wasn't, I'd a run his tail away!"

Lillie's youngest son, Massie, passed away in 1984. Audrey, Frank, and Norman still live at the homeplace, close to Lillie, and Roy lives in Waynesboro. In addition to her five children, Lillie now has thirteen grandchildren, sixteen great-grandchildren, and two great-great-grandchildren. She's led a full life on the farm where she and her beloved husband lived for nearly seventy-five years, just a stone's throw way from where they were both born and raised.

In today's transient world, there are only a few people who can boast that accomplishment. Like many of the older generation, Lillie says that folks nowadays don't have the pleasure of visiting and are too busy always going somewhere. I'd like to take the time to thank Lillie for reminding us that the simple things of life are still the most important after all.

Taken from the April 2003 *Backroads*

Clyde Carter at his Sherando homeplace

17

Clyde Carter

Sherando, Virginia

For the people in our immediate area, the man in the photograph to the left has been a familiar face in *Backroads* over the years. Clyde Carter is one of the few people who continue to live in the same community he was born and raised in. He has no desire to be anywhere else and says he's led a full life and has always been satisfied in the tiny village of Sherando.

Soft spoken and slight of build, Clyde is considered a man of few words. He has worked hard all his eighty-three years and is much loved and respected by family and friends. I have always appreciated the way he invited me into his home to share with *Backroads* readers what his early life was like.

Clyde was born on August 6, 1914, the second child of thirteen born to Robert and Nettie Patterson Carter of Sherando. All thirteen children, from eldest to youngest, are as follows: Halcie, Clyde, Lawrence, Racie, Charles Thomas (who died in infancy), Garfield, Manola, Edith, Onie, Wilbur, Jean, Bobby, and Ann.

In October 1997, at the time of this writing, eleven of the children are still living, and nine live in the area.

Clyde's father was a timber man, cutting trees for a living. He sawed wood for railroad ties and hauled them by horse and wagon to the Lyndhurst railway depot where they were then shipped to different destinations. Clyde said he was about five years old when he started accompanying his father to the woods and about eight or nine years of age when he started helping with the physical work. He remembers using a cross-cut saw to cut timber and using horses to skid the logs out.

Clyde's mama stayed home, tended to the children, and handled the work around the house that constantly needed doing with a family that large. Clyde put it rather succinctly by saying, "Mama had her hands full!"

The first house Clyde remembers his family living at was located in the little lane that ran behind the Emmett Davis home, where Maphis Henderson now lives. The Carters owned a lot of land along what is now Route 610. Clyde lived at home until he was twenty-six.

He began dating a girl by the name of Lucille Noe, whose family was originally from West Virginia but had moved to Sherando. He and Lucille courted and later married on June 12, 1940, at the Lutheran church parsonage in Ladd. The newlyweds lived with her family for about a month before going out on their own and renting a small cabin near where Hugh Coffey had his country store at the rock station on Route 664.

In 1947, the Carters bought twenty-one acres of land from a Mr. Paxton in Sherando and built a house along Back Creek on the unpaved wagon road off the Howardsville Turnpike. Clyde went to work at Wayne Manufacturing Company, which was located in Waynesboro, the closest town to Sherando. He worked as a shear operator, cutting sheet metal, starting out at thirty-two cents an hour, which he said was good money back then.

The Carters did not get electricity in their home until the 1950s, so Clyde would milk the family cow in the morning and take the milk to the closest spring to keep it cold. He's always had a fondness for pigs and has kept them on his place ever since living here. The family would butcher a beef cow and hogs each fall.

Clyde and Lucille had five children: Clyde Jr., Donna, Sheryl, Larry, and Fonda. Fonda stayed with her parents until the 1960s when she found employment at Morton Frozen Foods in Crozet.

Clyde retired from Wayne Manufacturing in March 1978; after retirement, he continued to work for his close friend, Grover Tomes, who owned a linoleum business.

Grover, Clyde, and Maynard Patterson were big coon hunting buddies. Clyde said that when the season came in, "We put everything else aside." Clyde remembers the season started on October 15 on private land and on November 15 on government land and lasted well into January. Clyde's best tree dog was a blue tick hound by the name of Simon that Clyde said would tree every time. The men would hunt anywhere from Highland County over to the James River and stay out all night for the sheer fun of the chase.

Clyde as a young man in 1942, holding one of his children

A Patterson hog butchering; Clyde at the left of the carcass

Clyde's wife Lucille passed away in 1996, but his five children, fourteen grandchildren, and seven great-grandchildren continue to visit him regularly. In fact, Clyde Jr. and Larry live with their father, and Larry recalled his wonderful childhood. "My mom and dad were real good to us, and we are a close family. Everyone is just a good bunch of folks."

These days, Clyde has slowed down a bit, but he continues to keep several sows and a boar hog. The day I visited him, I got to walk up to the barn and watch a dozen little fat piglets running around the lot where he keeps them. It's a nice quiet place along Back Creek, and it's easy to understand Clyde when he says, "I've had a full life here."

Taken from the October 1997 *Backroads*

Saylor Allen; Stuarts Draft, Virginia

Sherando Lake and rock bathhouse in the early years

18

Sherando Lake

U. S. Forest Service Recreational Area

In February 1934, the hearty men of the 351st Civilian Conservation Corps, based in Sherando, Virginia, began clearing the lakebed for a new recreational area that the U. S. Forest Service was slated to build. The park, which was going to be called the Sherando Lake Recreational Area, was part of a thirty thousand–acre game refuge called Big Levels, located in the George Washington National Forest.

Building the road to the lake

The dam and spillway in the spring of 1935 after
a November 1934 flood ripped out the right side of the dam

The twenty-one-acre lake, fed by spring water and formed by an earthen dam 207 feet in length, sloped off from a sandy beach built for wading and swimming to a twenty-foot depth at the dam.

The work continued until July 1, 1936, and the government's plan was that they would have the new recreational area open to the public in time for the July 4 opening of the Shenandoah National Park. A large dedication service was being held at Shenandoah Park, and President Roosevelt would be in attendance. Officials were hoping to open Sherando Lake in conjunction with the National Park just twenty miles away.

Although the lake was not entirely finished, some twenty-five hundred visitors came for the Fourth of July holiday. The men from the CCC Camp served as lifeguards on the sparkling sandy beach they had constructed just a few years previously.

Hours set for the new facility were weekdays from 4:30 p.m. until 7:30 p.m., Saturdays from 1:30 p.m. until 7:30 p.m., and Sundays and holidays from 10:00 a.m. until 7:30 p.m. Use of the recreational area was limited to swimming, boating, and picnicking. At this time, the stone bathhouse had not been constructed and facilities for camping were not in effect. The water system would come much later in the project, and those using the area had to provide their own refreshments.

In a newspaper article that ran Friday, May 28, 1937, under the caption "Your Questions about Sherando Lake Answered," there were some interesting queries concerning the recreational area. How deep is the water? How wide is the lake? How big is the dam? Anticipating the need for answers to these and other questions about nearby Sherando Lake Forest Camp, the *News-Virginian* published pertinent information about the lake; the answers to questions were supplied by R. F. Knoth, assistant in education and information, U. S. Forest Service office at Harrisonburg, Virginia. Mr. Knoth regularly writes the "Say, Ranger?" column for the *News-Virginian*. Facts about the lake are as follows:

Area of lake, 21 acres

Maximum width, 500 feet

Maximum length, 1,800 feet

Maximum depth, 27 feet

Elevation at crest of dam, 2,031 feet

Elevation at water level, 2,022 feet

Elevation at spillway floor, 2,018.5 feet

Elevation at top flashboards, 2,022 feet

Height of flashboards, 3 feet 6 inches

Length of dam, 236 feet

Width of dam at top, 8 feet 6 inches

Width of dam at base, 218 feet

Length of spillway, 140 feet

Width of spillway, 35 feet

Cubic feet of earth in dam, 40,800

Cubic yards of concrete in spillway, 950

Height of gate tower, 35 feet

An early sign into Sherando Lake

An aerial view of the lake after it was opened

Development continued on the area until its final completion in 1938. The park was closed during World War II and reopened and rededicated in August 1946. Because of an increase in population, expansion and development of a new camping area and other facilities continued well up into the 1960s.

Today, the lake is still as pristine as the day it opened. The campsites are wooded and set off by themselves, and the lake is still spring-fed by the cold, clear mountain streams. The open-air amphitheater is used on a regular basis for entertainment by those camping at Sherando Lake, and there are numerous trails for the hiking enthusiasts. Trout streams abound in the recreational area, and they are well stocked during fishing season. The lake is also a favorite spot for locals who just want to come and enjoy it for an afternoon. For those who just want to get away from it all, there are plenty of shady spots where one can stretch out and do a bit of relaxing.

Many people over the years have benefited from the U. S. Forest Service's plan to construct this recreational area in a deep hollow against a backdrop of the Blue Ridge Mountains. The Service's foresight and with the men from the 351st Civilian Conservation Corps, who provided much of the labor to complete the project, have opened up numerous ways for people to get out in the great outdoors, and we thank them for preserving this special gift of nature for all to enjoy.

Portions taken from the July 1986 *Backroads*

Margie Hatter at her home in Tyro

19

Margie Coffey Hatter

Tyro, Virginia

I first met Margie and her husband, Junior, on July 4, 1980. We had taken our Love neighbors, Johnny and Nin Coffey, for an auto trip down the North Fork of the Tye River from Montebello to Nash, and we stopped at Hatter's Goodwill Grocery. We went in for a cold drink and sat down in the chairs at the back of the store where the locals congregated and began talking. I remember thinking how hospitable they both were and how much I liked them.

In 1981, I began singing with a little gospel group; Margie invited us over to White Rock to sing for the Ramsey reunion. The reunion, which is a combination of Ramsey, Coffey, Allen, Steele, and assorted other family tree branches, is always held on the last Sunday of July at the old Eli Coffey cabin. Eli was the father of Hercy Coffey, and Margie was the firstborn of three daughters born to Hercy and Lora Burgess Ramsey Coffey, who was featured in *Backroads 2: The Road to Chicken Holler*.

The little community of White Rock is located on Route 687, and the cold, clear waters of the North fork of the Tye River flow alongside it. It is one of the prettiest places here in the mountains, and I've been blessed to have attended many a function along its beautiful banks. Margie and her two sisters, Lura and Lorine, were raised in this idyllic spot and never left it until after marriage. Lorine and her husband, Glenn Allen, now own the property where Eli's cabin and Hercy and Burgess's home stands.

After *Backroads* newspaper started in December 1981, Margie began calling me to ask if I'd be interested in doing a story on something she felt was newsworthy. I've lost count of all the articles I wrote in *Backroads* because of her prompting. She always seemed to be in the middle of some pretty neat goings-on that I thought were terrific. If it weren't for her, I'm not sure I would have ever gotten to meet people like Teressie Coffey, Maggie Allen, Ethna and Wilson Seaman, Maxie and Mary Seaman, Annie Carr, Lena Zirkle, and many other mountain people I was privileged to interview over the years.

Margie took me on countless impromptu picnics up the North Fork and beyond. One morning, she called to tell me to come over because she was taking me to a class reunion at Mill Creek School. I remember riding in the back seat of her Jeep with the aroma of hot ham biscuits and fresh apple pie surrounding my senses and making me hungry for lunch at ten o'clock in the morning. She pulled up to Billy Morris's house, and the preacher came hopping out in his stocking feet to see what was going on. After a few minutes, and now shod, he came out again and climbed into the Jeep, balancing a big pot of North Carolina field peas and fatback on his lap. We wound our way through the mountains to a pristine one-room schoolhouse tucked deep in a hollow between Dowell's Ridge and Montebello. Ten older people were waiting for us. These were some of the "children" who had attended Mill Creek School over the years, since it had been established in 1904. We ate, we visited, we sang, and I took many pictures which accompanied the Mill Creek School reunion article that ran in the November 1984 issue of *Backroads*.

In September of that same year, I dedicated one whole newspaper to the tiny community of White Rock and once again went on a picnic up to Eli Coffey's cabin with Margie and a bunch of her family members, who were kind enough to give me information for the special issue. Margie herself told this story:

> Junior and I got married in 1942, and he left for the service that fall. After he came back, we traveled around a good bit. We lived in West Virginia, Maryland, and in Vir-

Margie and Junior on the porch of their store

ginia; we lived in Clifton Forge and Lexington for a while.

In 1946, we came back to Tyro and bought a little piece of land from Junior's father. It had a little store on it that was closed up, but we fixed it up and reopened that spring. It had a house in the rear and we lived there until 1956. We decided to move after a series of small floods kept making a mess of things. We were forever mopping up the mud and water after one of these storms, since the store was located on the banks of the Tye River. So we bought a piece of property across from the store that was on higher ground and built our home there. Junior was a mail carrier from about 1962 until he had to retire because of

The Hatter's Goodwill Grocery in Tyro

a bad back. We had a good life, and everything in it was pretty normal. We never had children of our own, but we took in a homeless boy by the name of Phillip Greene when he was eleven years old, and Martin Bradley made his home with us off and on since he was a teenager.

We have seen a lot of different changes here since we've been running the store. I guess one of the biggest ones occurred in 1969. That was the year of the big flood. Hurricane Camille had devastated Mississippi, and I remember watching all the flood damage on television. I remarked how awful it would be if it ever hit here. Little did I realize that that very night Camille would rip through this hollow and destroy not only the land, but people's lives as well.

It was cloudy all day and around seven o'clock that evening, it started to rain. I never saw such rain! It made me real nervous, and I couldn't get to sleep. About one o'clock in the morning, I looked out the window and told Junior to come and look. The river was coming right down the middle of the road and our car was being washed away. We got scared and decided to take Phillip and head up the steep mountain behind our house. It rained all night, with continuous lightning and thunder that was deafening. When it started to get light, we came down off the mountain and could not believe the devastation. Our store was completely gone, but miraculously our home was still standing. We were one of the lucky ones . . . all we lost was our livelihood, not our lives.

We took in boarders from the men who came in to work on the road and managed to support ourselves. If it wasn't for the Mennonites who came to help us, we probably would never have been able to rebuild the store. They came [from] as far away as Pennsylvania to help us. Slowly we began to get on our feet again, and in 1971, the Hatter's Goodwill Grocery opened its doors. We renamed it that because if it wasn't for the good will of the Mennonites, we would never have been able to start over.

In the September 1984 White Rock edition of *Backroads*, Margie Hatter submitted a poem she had written about Hurricane Camille entitled "The Nelson County Flood." In her own words, the poem reflects the total devastation that happened the night of August 19, 1969, for not only her family but countless others who lived in Nelson at that time. When the first Backroads book came out, Margie's sisters, Lura Steele and Lorine Allen, came to our cabin to purchase one. Their eyes welled up with tears when they saw the front cover photograph taken from 20 Minute Cliff, which shows the Tye River Valley below. Lorine pointed to the tiny white speck in the photo that was their house and said, "This is where we came the day after the flood to see if our house was still standing. . . ."

Margie (left) with her sisters, Lorine and Lura

The Nelson County Flood

It was August 19th in the year of '69,
The day was very dark, and the sun didn't shine.
The clouds hung low and the day was drear,
And people didn't realize that death was near.

It was around the hour of 8:00 p.m.,
When a storm called Camille came pouring in.
The lightning lashed, the thunder roared,
For around eight hours the rain did pour.

In the morning hours, just before dawn,
The flood came down, our loved ones gone.
The rocks, the trees, and the mountains fell down,
Many were buried beneath the ground.

Part of some families were left alive,
Some were hanging in trees and managed to survive.
While many were swept away that night,
They did not live to see daylight.

Little children were taken from their parents' arms,
Where they could no longer protect them from harm.
They were swept away in the muddy water,
They were gone forever from Mother and Father.

When daylight came to them that survived,
They wondered how many loved ones had died.
But there was no way for them to know,
There was no communication . . . not even a road.

Many people prayed to God above,
To save their lives and the ones they loved.
Some prayers were answered, and some were not,
For we cannot weigh the will of God.

Nelson County was torn apart,
The houses, the highways, and everyone's heart.
No one will forget that stormy night,
And the deep rolling waters before daylight.

For me, the years came and went with a deepening friendship
with Margie and her sweet family. There were reunions, birthdays
and anniversaries, special events at Cornerstone Church where she

attended, and impromptu picnics along the North Fork. I guess the saddest times I spent with her was when we buried her dear mother and beloved husband in 1993 and 1995, respectively. Then came the day in May 1999 that I stood off to myself, watching six men bear the weight of her casket as they laid Margie to rest in the Hatter family graveyard, just a few feet from the rock home where she lived.

Junior sneaking a kiss on their fiftieth wedding anniversary

The memories I have of her are tucked in the forever part of my heart that holds the most precious of God's gifts, and one day, in the sweet by and by, those memories will be rekindled as we spend an eternity catching up. . . .

Portions taken from the September 1984 *Backroads*

The Fork Mountain Girls; Ethel, Velma, and Mabel

20

The Fork Mountain Girls

Ethel, Velma, and Mabel Fitzgerald; Montebello, Virginia

One day I received a phone call from a Backroads reader saying I ought to interview an older woman by the name of Ethel Matheny, who knew the early history of the Fork Mountain area. Over the years, I had talked to Ethel on the phone, and she always seemed very pleasant. So I called her one evening to ask about doing a story in the newspaper. By the end of the conversation, I knew I had hit pay dirt. Ethel said she had two sisters, Velma and Mabel Ramsey, who were willing to come and share their memories of growing up together on Fork Mountain and also bring some early family photographs to go along with the article in *Backroads*. This would be the first time I interviewed three sisters at the same time, and it was hard to tell who was the most excited, they or I.

After I arrived at Ethel's home in Stuarts Draft and met all three of the "Fork Mountain Girls," I realized that Ethel was the mother of a friend of mine, Glenn Allen, and also the wife of Eugene "Hoot" Allen, who was the best friend of my neighbor, Johnny Coffey.

I can't express how much I enjoyed meeting these dear ladies, and it turned out to be one of the nicest afternoons I ever spent. I came away filled with the special kind of joy that comes from meeting kindred spirits, and I learned a lot of new things; such as, if you put some raw apple slices in with a stale cake, it puts the moisture

back in! So set back for a spell and read how things were on Fork
Mountain when Ethel, Velma, and Mabel were growing up.

Alfred McElroy Fitzgerald and Lelia Burgess Bradley Fitzgerald
were both seventeen years old when they wed on Valentine's Day,
1896. Although they were young, the couple had twenty-two
happy years together before Lelia died of Bright's disease when she
was thirty-nine. Five daughters and two sons were born to the
Fitzgeralds: Lottie Burgess, Lula Pearl, William Boyd, Lora Ethel,
Henry Claibourne, Ollie Velma, and Dura Mabel.

The Fitzgerald family lived out on Fork Mountain, near the
village of Montebello, in the homeplace that had belonged to several generations before them. The Fitzgeralds, like so many of the
mountain people, were of Scottish/Irish descent, the family having emigrated in the 1700s. Ethel, Velma, and Mabel's great-
grandfather, Henry Ruffner Fitzgerald, was a Baptist minister,
schoolteacher, and early photographer for that area.

The three sisters held special memories of growing up on one of
the oldest homesteads on Fork Mountain. Their daddy was a
farmer who saw to it that his family's basics were taken care of by
raising everything they needed right on the farm. Items such as
shoes, coffee, and sugar were bought with the cash that was earned
by selling their excess garden produce, eggs, and chestnuts. The
sisters' mother saw to it that her children had warm clothing, blan-
kets, and heavy socks she made from sheep's wool on the spinning
wheel and family loom. In the summer months, the children slept
on straw tick mattresses, switching to warm feather tick comforters
in the winter. The ticks were emptied in the fall and spring; the
material was washed and then restuffed with sweet-smelling straw
from the fields and newly plucked down from the geese and ducks
that were kept on the farm.

Everyone had their own chores to do. The girls said they would
scrub the oak floor in the kitchen with water and a broom, sweep
it out the door, and let the floor dry to a bleached-bone white. In
the evenings, after the supper dishes were done, the women pieced
quilts or did some knitting while the men played music before it
was time to retire for the night. At five o'clock in the morning,

the whirring sound of the hand-cranked coffee grinder would wake them, and the wonderful aroma of fresh coffee would bring them running to the kitchen for breakfast.

Large fields of rye and buckwheat were raised, and each year at harvest time the threshing crews would come to help gather in the grain. Beans were planted in the corn rows and brought to the barn to dry. Once dried, the beans would be "frailed out" (beaten with a stick) to remove the beans from the pods. They were then picked up for storage or sold if the family needed items from the store.

The Fitzgerald home had a large room downstairs, along with three bedrooms plus a darkroom where their great-grandfather kept all of his photography equipment. The upstairs was all one big room used for sleeping purposes. There was a detached kitchen with a connecting breezeway. The girls remember the kitchen as being a large room that held a long table with chairs, two pie safes, a fireplace, a wood cook stove, and a huge handmade cupboard that their great-grandfather had built to keep coffee, soda, and salt in. There were also two wooden barrels where flour and meal were kept. Even with all the furniture in the kitchen, there was still plenty of space for the children to play.

So the three Fitzgerald sisters grew up and went from rag dolls and rag curls to mature, beautiful young women who eventually married and had families of their own.

Ethel, like her parents before her, married Eugene Montgomery "Hoot" Allen when she was seventeen. They started out living at Eagle Rock, Virginia, then made a brief move to West Virginia; but because of health reasons, they moved back home and settled along the North Fork of the Tye River, near the community of White Rock. They were very happy and had five children together: Dennis, Glenn, Louise, Maxie, and Verna. Hoot died in 1952. In 1960, Ethel married another wonderful man by the name of Roy Matheny.

Mabel surpassed even her parents' young ages when she married Guy Maxwell Ramsey when she was fifteen years old. They also made several moves before settling down in the Vesuvius area, where she continues to live. The Ramseys had four children: Winfred, Edgar, Joyce, and Faye.

An early family photograph: (top row) Eunice (Alfred's sister) and Lottie;
(bottom row) William, Alfred, Ethel, Lelia with Clairborne on her lap, and Lula

Just when the family started to worry that Velma would be an old maid, she married Stanley Morgan Ramsey at the ripe old age of twenty. Velma and Stanley had two children: Eloise and Kenneth. They set a record number of moves (seventeen in all) before settling down close to Mabel and Maxie in Vesuvius. Stanley was Maxie's brother, so two Ramsey brothers married two Fitzgerald sisters.

The ladies are all alone now, all three widowed; but they still enjoy getting together with family and friends. Being with them is a delightful combination of love and laughter as they banter back and forth good naturedly. As the interview wound down, all three fussed over me, feeding me homemade cake and filling my coffee cup. Ethel took me into her bedroom and showed me some of her handiwork: afghans in different, brightly colored patterns and old-fashioned lace collars that were once again making a comeback.

Velma's daughter Eloise came in with her husband George Allen and their daughter Becky. Over the years, I had taken photographs of George and Becky, both top-notch bluegrass musicians, at all the family reunions, but I had never known that they were related to Velma. It always amazes me what a small world we live in.

As I gathered up my camera and notepad to leave, I thought about what a great day it had been. I was so grateful for the opportunity to meet and get to know Ethel, Velma, and Mabel . . . the Fork Mountain girls!

Taken from the March 1991 *Backroads*

Lisa Swisher opening gifts at her Montebello pounding

21

Poundings, Shivarees, and the Rain Crow

POUNDINGS

I had never heard of this old custom that was a big part of each mountain community years ago. In the early times, a "pounding" was given to each newly married couple just starting out in their own home, a family moving into a new cabin, or to welcome a new preacher. The idea was to help newcomers to fill their pantry with the essentials that every home needs. It was a party, of sorts, to which friends and family brought gifts such as flour, sugar, salt, coffee, and a variety of home-canned or baked goods. It was usually given by the neighbors or the members of the church where the couple attended. The term "pounding" was used because the gifts were all in weights, as in five pounds of sugar, a pound of salt, etc.

The first pounding I ever attended was for Tinker and Barbara Kiser of Stuarts Draft, Virginia. The young couple had just bought and renovated the old Bill Bradley home on Flory Avenue, and the ladies of Mountain View Mennonite Church, where I attended, told me about the custom and invited me to be a part of it. I rode to the Kisers' home with Gladys Coffey, and she's the one who filled me in on what a pounding actually was. I remember Gladys gave the couple a beautiful eight-sided star quilt hanging that she had made for their home, along with some of her delicious homemade jelly. In addition to the various food items, the Kisers also received potholders, washcloths, coffee mugs, trivets, and towels.

Louise and Lyle Bradley with a colorful quilt that they received at their pounding

The members of Mount Paran Baptist Church where my husband, Billy, was preaching gave two other poundings. The first one was for Lisa Swisher, a single gal who had just moved to Montebello; the other was for Lyle and Louise Bradley, who had roots in the same area and had moved back from Gloucester, Virginia. Like the Kisers, Lisa, Lyle, and Louise were showered with not only the "necessities" of a standard pounding but also many lovely gifts for the home.

This is a wonderful tradition that continues to be carried on in our locale and one I hope will pass down to future generations.

Taken from the March 1985 and July 2001 *Backroads*

SHIVAREES

"Mr. Webster" says that a shivaree is a mock serenade made by blowing horns, beating on pans, and ringing cowbells, often as a practical joke played on newly married couples.

The custom is thought to have begun in the Middle Ages, and there are many variations on the way it is conducted. It is an old custom that seems to have died out in today's sophisticated culture, but in years past, in the Blue Ridge Mountains, it played a significant part in people's idea of fun.

A group of friends would go over to the newlyweds' home, preferably late at night when the couple was already asleep, and proceed to march around the house in a noisy demonstration. Cowbells, shotgun blasts, and pot banging continued until the couple came out on the porch and kissed in front of the raucous crowd. If the crowd was particularly rambunctious, they might "kidnap" the bride or make the groom do a bit of foolishness.

Shivaree essentials: cow bells, pots, wooden spoons, and a lantern to light the way

Johnny Coffey said that one night, some of the mountain folks got together and shivareed Royal and Sadie Everitt, who had gotten married and were living in a log cabin on top of the hill near Love. "We all made a lot of noise and went 'round and 'round the house," recalled Johnny. He added, "On the way home, we decided to shivaree George Demastus, too. Old George was a bachelor, you know, so we thought it would be a pretty good joke on him. But the joke turned out to be on us that night because after all the fuss we made, it turned out George wasn't even home!"

And I recall Roy Kiser saying that when he and Charlene had gotten married, the rabble-rousers came to their home and "kidnapped" Roy and made him ride a board around the house before they would let him go.

Although I have not had the pleasure of being a part of an actual shivaree here on the mountain, it would be something to tuck in the back of my mind, just in case there is an occasion to have one!

Taken from the October 1983 *Backroads*

THE RAIN CROW

I had lived in the small mountain hamlet of Love, Virginia, for at least ten years before finally identifying an unusual sound that came from the woods near our cabin. The sound started in the warm summer months, and it sounded like a cross between a frog and a bird. It made a series of low, mournful, quivering cries that sounded like "shoo-lump, shoo-lump."

I told Manley Allen about the strange sound, and he asked what I thought it was. I told him maybe it was some type of bird, but I couldn't be sure. He laughed and said it was a "rain crow," and I thought for sure he was pulling my leg. But then I ran into Maynard Patterson at our country grocery, and he told me the same thing. A few days later, he handed me a newspaper clipping about the bird. The clipping told all about the haunting song of the bird mountain people called the "rain crow."

The bird in question is a Black-billed Cuckoo. In North America there are two types of cuckoos: black-billed and yellow-billed. They are slender birds about a foot long and have long, rounded tails. Their feet are different from most birds in that two of their toes point forward and the other two backward. Their beaks are long and curved, and their coloring is an olive-brown on the back with a white breast.

The Black-billed Cuckoos make their homes in woods, thickets, and orchards. The nests are built in an untidy fashion, and two to seven eggs are laid in one nest.

The birds feed on insect pests such as hairy caterpillars that are shunned by other birds for one reason or another. Because they are strictly insect eaters, the cuckoos migrate to the tropics during the winter months. This explains why I have never heard their plaintive song in the wintertime.

The most fascinating trait that the Black-billed Cuckoo has, and the one that has earned them the name of "rain crow," is its uncanny ability to predict rain within twenty-four hours from the time you hear their cry. I've found that in the thirty years of living here in the Blue Ridge Mountains, the rain crow is much more accurate than the TV weather forecasters.

One summer day when our son Mike and a bunch of his buddies came roaring in on their motorcycles bound for a long day of riding, I asked if they had packed their rain suits. The day was clear and cloudless, so our son asked why they would need them on such a gorgeous day. I told him I heard the rain crow's cry that morning while working in the garden, so most likely they'd need them before the day was over. Everyone had a good laugh at my odd prediction, but later that night, Mike called and said, "Well, you and the rain crow were right . . . we all got soaked!" You can't improve on Mother Nature.

Taken from the April 1988 *Backroads*

Hallie Henderson on the porch of her home in Love

22

Hallie Quick Henderson

Love, Virginia

The following interview with Hallie appeared in the July 1982 *Backroads*; seven years later, when she passed away in March 1989, her grandson Marvin Henderson Jr. wrote a tribute to her in the June 1989 issue. The following is a combination of the two.

They say that big things come in small packages, and I've found that Hallie Henderson, long-time resident of the Love community, is no exception. This tough-minded mountain woman with the sweet disposition has all those "big things" tucked away inside her tiny, slender frame. Things like determination, perseverance, and pure spunk!

When I went down to interview Hallie, she was out on her front porch repotting flowers with a vengeance. She dusted off her hands, and we sat on the glider and talked about her life in general. I found out many things I never knew about her and came away that morning with a renewed respect for these plucky mountain people.

Widowed at thirty-two years of age, Hallie raised her three sons single handedly, trying to be both mother and father to them. Never having worked outside the home, she found herself faced with the total responsibility of the boys' upbringing after her husband, Odie, passed away.

Never missing a beat, she got a job at the Esmond Blanket Factory in Waynesboro and left her three children with her brother,

Sidney, while she worked the four to midnight shift. In the mornings, she arose early to get a start on the never-ending chores of a mountain homestead. She carried bucket after bucket of water from the spring and heated it on a woodstove for washing clothes, doing dishes, and taking baths. She split and hauled her own wood, raised her own hogs and chickens, tended a large vegetable garden, canned her winter food supply, and milked a farm cow twice a day. In the summer months, when there was time, she took the children blackberry picking.

Hallie said, "About the only rest and recreation we had was to walk to church on Sunday to listen to the preaching and later in the afternoon visit with the neighbors."

I asked if she ever got lonely or thought about remarriage, and she said, "Looking back, yes, it did get lonely at times, but there was so much work to be done that you had no time to dwell on it." As for remarriage, Hallie said it was her honest belief that the Lord gives you only one true love on this earth; she had had hers, and she didn't have any desire to start looking again. "Yes, child, times were hard. Why one time, we were down to literally our last crust of bread, but I never asked for help. I figured if the Lord wanted us to starve, then we'd all go together. But we never did. Something always came in, and the Lord provided for us. A neighbor would come over with a meal, or I'd get some extra money somehow," explained Hallie.

Hallie's home in Love, Virginia

After sixteen years of hard work, Hallie had saved up enough money to buy the house she lives in today. It is a neat, white farmhouse that sits back in a shady spot at the foot of the mountain. That house has a history all its own. The timber used to build it came from the old Dunkard Church, up the road about a mile, across from where Ralph Hewitt lives. According to Mr. Johnny Coffey, at one time the church boasted so many members that on "baptizing Sunday" (usually held in August when the church homecoming occurred), you could see white-robed people lined up and down the narrow dirt road waiting their turn to be immersed in the cold, clear water of Back Creek.

Today, Hallie lives the same type of simple lifestyle that she always has, minus a lot of the hardships of earlier times. She still fetches water in from the spring for washing dishes and bathing, tends a large garden, and brings in the wood that her sons keep cut for her for the woodstove. About the only thing that has changed is the path to the privy, which now leads across the road to her son Marvin's house. "It's a lot warmer over there," laughs Hallie.

Hallie showing off her spring

Later on the morning of our interview, Hallie took me out back and proudly showed me the spring which had supplied her with fresh water all these years. It lay at the foot of the mountain in the shade of her backyard. The crystal clear water lay undisturbed in its natural stone basin. At Hallie's insistence, I reached over and took the dipper hanging on a tree limb, filled it with the cold liquid, and took a sip.

"Honey, that there is some of the best water you'll ever drink in these parts," Hallie was saying as I finished up my dipperful.

As I passed her the cup, I noticed what appeared to be a small water snake coiled up at the bottom of the spring. "I can see what gives it that distinctive flavor," I teased, as I lifted the half frozen snake up to the surface.

"Mercy child," screamed Hallie, "Now where in the world did *that* thing come from?"

I almost got the poor snake out of the spring before it fell off the stick and slid back into the water to hide among the rocks. We had a great laugh over it, and she assured me that her son, Marvin, would get it out of there the very first chance he got. I left that morning feeling extremely happy inside and vowed to apologize to Marvin the very first chance *I* got!

MY GRANDMOTHER, HALLIE HENDERSON
By *Marvin Henderson, Jr.*

Love Mountain is a great place to live. Many have been raised on the mountain and some have left. But some have lived their entire lives there. My grandmother, Hallie Henderson, was born in Nelson County in the Blue Ridge Mountains and moved at an early age to the Augusta County side and settled on Love Mountain. She died on March 25, 1989, but the many memories I have of her will never die.

Grandma Henderson was a small woman in size but a very big woman in heart. If ever a woman deserved a heavenly crown for hard work and dedication, it was her. When my grandfather Odie Henderson was in his early thirties, he died, leaving her with three sons. Joe was fourteen, Melvin was just five years of age, and my dad, Marvin, was only thirteen months old. Grandma told me many times of folks who wanted to take her sons away, but she vowed that the only way they would take them was over her dead body. Always a hard worker, she raised all three boys by herself.

Grandma loved many things typical of mountain life. I remember the many times we sat down and ate our favorite meal together . . . squirrel legs and gravy. She was proud of the many pots of flowers she kept on her front porch for all to see. I have seen her working in her precious garden many an early morning, wearing her customary ankle-length dress. She never did have running water in her home. An ever-flowing spring at the bottom of the ridge behind her house was the only source of water.

Grandma was a true believer in God. She was always in church on Sunday mornings in her favorite end seat on the fourth row back. Many times I remember seeing the large-print edition of the New Testament in the house where she had been reading. She loved to quilt and play her old pump organ before arthritis limited her from doing either. She never learned how to drive, although she did confess to driving an old Model T Ford one time.

Hallie on her front porch

Most of all, I remember the true mountain wisdom of Grandma Henderson. She always let you know where she stood on any issue. One thing she said that always stuck with me was, "When choosing a wife, it ain't like horses and cows . . . you can't just get rid of them when you don't want them."

It was a sunny day with a slight breeze on the twenty-fifth of March when she was laid beneath the hemlocks at Mountain View Mennonite Church Cemetery. It was just the kind of day Grandma would have loved!

"Who can find a virtuous woman?
For her price is far above rubies."

—Proverbs 31:10

Frosty and Hester, still in love after sixty–five years of marriage

23

Frosty and Hester Brooks

Steeles Tavern, Virginia

N ot many couples can make the claim that they've spent an entire lifetime together as Frosty and Hester Brooks can. This couple, who celebrated their sixty-fifth anniversary in July 2003, has never known a day they weren't together.

They were born three days apart, and their families lived within spitting distance of one another in the little settlement of Pkin, just up the road from Vesuvius. They grew up toddling around as tiny children, playing together, courting in their teen years, and marrying when they were both nineteen years old.

Forest Purcival "Frosty" Brooks was born on July 3, 1919, the second child of Euley Hewitt Brooks and Ora Houser Brooks. He came by his unique nickname because another boy in the area was named Forest Brooks, so they dubbed Forest Purcival "Frosty" to indicate which Forest they

Courtesy of Frosty Brooks

Frosty as an infant

were talking about. The other boy died early, but by then Frosty's nickname had stuck, and he carried it throughout the rest of his life. There were seven other children born to the Brooks family—four boys: Hewett, Bruce, Gray, and Buryl; and three girls: Millie (Potter), Evelyn (Sensabaugh), and Bential (Groah).

Euley worked at the rock crushing plant close to their home. Frosty remembered his father coming home each evening covered with white dust. Euley eventually contracted TB and died at thirty-eight years of age. Even though Frosty's mother was there to raise the younger children, Frosty quit school to help take care of his youngest sister, Bential, who was born two months after their father died.

Hester Almond Bradley was born on July 6, 1919, the eldest daughter of Eugene Bradley and Rena Anderson Bradley. Hester had five sisters: Lola, who died in infancy, Frances (Heizer), Betty (Harris), Annie (Johnson), and Mary Carmelitius "Dickie" (Kemp); and one brother, Lewis. Hester, like Frosty, quit school in the fourth grade to take care of her younger siblings when her mother fell ill and died at forty years of age.

Hester said she learned how to make bread, standing on a metal box to reach the table. She washed on a washboard and took on all the responsibly of raising a family at fourteen years of age. Her father hired out for farm work and worked as a railroad laborer at Vesuvius, laying track and railroad ties by hand. The families both lived on five acres of land apiece and kept cows for milk, chickens for meat and eggs, and hogs for fall butchering. Hester said she and her sister, Frances, walked the two miles to Edgar Austin's store in Vesuvius and carried bags of groceries home on their backs.

While they were still attending school, Frosty and Hester both walked to the two-room Pkin School (known as the Cotopaxi School before that time) a few miles from their homes, which offered first- through seventh-grade classes. They both remember one teacher named Miss Garber who boarded with the Bob Ham family and ended up marrying Bob's son, Raleigh. The Bradleys and the Brooks also walked to Mount Joy Presbyterian Church, which was located two miles from their homes, and they said they

The Pkin School

Pkin School pupils in 1929; Frosty is standing on the far right

had to cross several rivers on foot logs on the way. There was a Preacher Boyle, who pastored the church and, although he had an automobile, walked everywhere to visit his parishioners. They said he kept a written logbook of dates for everyone he called on or shared a meal with.

It was a natural thing for the young couple to court and marry when they were older. When asked when she knew she loved Frosty, Hester smiled and said, "The first time I laid eyes on him."

Frosty, in turn, said he knew he loved
Hester when he was "knee high to a
duck." They were married at the
Vesuvius Baptist Church parsonage
on July 5, 1938, right in between each
of their birthdays. Frosty turned nineteen on July 3, and Hester turned
nineteen on the sixth, the day after
their marriage. Rev. Dow McGrady
performed the ceremony when it was
learned that Preacher Boyle would be
away on that day. But on the next
available Sunday, Frosty and Hester

Frosty and Hester as a teenage couple

went to church and dedicated themselves as a couple, to always
serve the Lord Jesus and bring up their children in a Christian
home.

Their honeymoon had to wait for a while since the night of
their wedding, Frosty had to return to the Civilian Conservation
Corps camp where he was employed. He served in the CCC in
West Virginia and in Virginia at Luray, Mount Solon, and Wool-
wine. Hester set up housekeeping in the upstairs rooms of her
father's house. When Frosty returned for good, they rented places
in Pkin, Greenville, and Spottswood where they lived on a farm,
doing general farm work such as digging thistles for ten cents an
hour, thinking they were making good money.

By this time, three children had been born to the Brookses:
Rosalee; Forest, Jr. "Bud"; and Kenneth.

In 1945, the family bought their first home for $875.00, where
they have lived ever since. The one-acre property came with a run
down, 1800s two-over-two style, three-story log home that was
supposedly haunted. When asked if they had ever heard any
strange goings-on, both told stories of curtains flapping, doors flying open for no apparent reason, and the sound of something
falling down the enclosed upstairs stairway. Upon inspection,
nothing was ever found. Frosty said that's probably why they
bought the property so cheap! If the house is indeed haunted, the

ghosts have been friendly and not malicious. Their last child, Richard, was born in this house. All the children were delivered at home by midwife Daisy Snead, who charged twenty-five dollars per child. They slowly fixed up the old home, adding several more rooms over the years. The house is located on Route 11 at Steele's Tavern, which the older folks called "Midway" because it is midway between Staunton and Lexington, Vesuvius and Raphine. Frosty said the road was only two lanes back then and was a wooden plank road in earlier years.

One of their early neighbors, Lonnie Helms, was an undertaker whom people called on for everything from making coffins and embalming corpses to hauling the body to the graveyard in his white hearse.

Frosty found better employment, first at Wayne Manufacturing in Waynesboro and then at Crompton Fabric Company, from which he retired in 1981 at sixty-two years of age and with thirty-six years of service. Hester has always been a homemaker, taking care of her family and also keeping other people's children in her home after hers were grown. Children have always been

An early Brooks family photograph

her first love, and she said that if she weren't in her eighties, she'd still be keeping them. Hester has made many beautiful quilts and still loves to read and work any type of crossword puzzle. For years, Frosty played the part of Santa Claus at many preschools, churches, and community centers during the holiday season. He also loved to coon hunt, keeping redbone hounds to hunt with. He and his buddy Clarence Lunsford loved nothing better than to take the dogs into the woods at night, lie on their backs in the leaves, and listen to the "night music" made by the treeing hounds.

These days, the Brookses lead busy, active lives, often leaving home early in the morning and not returning until late afternoon. They volunteer their time, visiting area hospitals and nursing homes, comforting those who are sick and alone, and entertaining

Frosty and Hester's fiftieth wedding anniversary

them as well. Frosty and Hester have both kept their keen sense of humor. Recently, when their son Richard called and asked his father, who was out of breath when he answered the phone, what he had been doing, Frosty replied, "Your mother and I are taking a little exercise, son." What Frosty didn't tell his son was that he and Hester had been dancing up a storm in the kitchen!

We salute you, Frosty and Hester Brooks. May your wonderful life together continue for many more years as an inspiration for the rest of us.

Taken from the December 2003 *Backroads*

Mattie Campbell; Roanoke, Virginia

Fresh-picked and canned green beans at the Coffey cabin

24

Gardening

Planting, Cultivating, Harvesting,
and Preserving Homegrown Foods

One of the most satisfying tasks I've had since moving to Virginia is raising my own vegetables in a home-garden plot. Gardening requires a lot of time and effort, but the rewards far outweigh any negatives involved in "digging in the dirt."

I grew up in south Florida, so my only exposure to gardening was my dad's planting of fruit trees in the back yard and an occasional watermelon patch. Although we never lacked oranges, limes, lemons, grapefruit, and bananas, vegetables grown in the Floridian sandy soil didn't do very well. It wasn't until I started cultivating the rocky ground in Love, Virginia, that I realized what the term "pay dirt" really meant. Vegetables seem to thrive in the earth here, and although I've picked enough field rocks off our property to rival the Great Wall of China, each year there is a fresh batch waiting when the plowing is done.

In recent years, I've noticed people in town growing tomatoes in flowerpots or digging up portions of their backyard, planting the "victory gardens" of the past to have fresh vegetables right outside their door. The harvest is fresh, convenient, and money saving to boot!

If you're fortunate to have a little land, the gardens get bigger. Each spring I say to my husband, Billy, "Let's cut down the size of our plot this year. . . . We don't need all this food." But then we take into consideration our deer and rabbit population, five married children and six grandkids, and sharing with friends and neighbors, and our plot becomes larger than it was the year before. We certainly don't waste the harvest; I can anything that moves around here and our pantry shelves are full, along with boxes stacked up on the floor. Billy swears the side of the cabin where the pantry is located is going to collapse one of these days!

Any serious gardener knows what I am talking about when I use the word "obsessive." I am positively anal when it comes to

A well-kept, early summer garden

preserving food, especially the canning part. I line the pantry shelves with colorful fruits and vegetables that I hate to use until winter officially comes, usually around Thanksgiving. In the early spring, when the larder gets low, I move the last jars to the front of the shelf, putting the empty pint and quart jars behind. The facade gives the impression there's an endless supply of foodstuffs. As I said . . . *obsessive!*

But there is something so amazing about sitting down to a meal you've prepared from your own garden. It struck me the first time I served a supper of baked Kennebec potatoes, fresh roasting ears, sliced tomatoes, and brown beans straight from the good earth. Everything tasted so much better, especially with a pan of hot biscuits smeared with some of Billy's honey taken from his beehives and a glass of thick buttermilk. You can't get any better than this.

I didn't start out being militant about organic gardening, but over the years it has just evolved. We used to spray with the best of them, trying to rid our plants of those pesky pests that seem to appear as soon as the vegetables do. But the more we dusted and sprayed, the hardier the bugs got. Then I received a book about the effects of the continual use of pesticides. It stated that pests become resistant to the poison, and one must keep changing the types of spray, using more and more, to get the same results. In the process, the poison also kills all the "good" bugs, such as praying mantises, true ladybugs, and even toads, which eat their fair share of garden pests. Because it takes longer for these to recover and make a comeback, the bad pests gain a foothold and take over. It's a vicious cycle that we decided to end. I began picking the potato bugs off by hand each morning, snipping off the leaves that had eggs laid on them. We called a local organics store that sold natural products and found a spay that actually worked to kill the pesky pests but didn't bother the "good" bugs. Also, someone told us that if you mix a little dishwashing liquid in a gallon of water and spray it liberally and often, it will work the same. That is on our list for this year's garden maintenance.

I have the mountain people to thank for teaching me what they knew about preserving homegrown food. They kept me from blowing myself up with the pressure cooker and showed me how to can large amounts of vegetables in a no. 2 washtub over an open fire. They passed on helpful hints to make the job go easier and were always just a phone call away if I got stuck and needed help. But I also learned a few new tricks from *Organic Gardening* magazine, given to me at Christmas by my former neighbor Jim Courtney. Jim was an organic gardener before they coined the phrase. He was the first person I ever knew who didn't use any kind of poisonous spray on his plants, and I gleaned a wealth of information from him about growing healthy, abundant crops.

During the last couple of years, the tips in the magazine have proved to be real time savers in the kitchen. Take, for instance, slicing corn off the cob. I always hated this job because the cobs would invariably slip out of my hand, I'd knick my finger with the knife, and the bits of corn would splatter everywhere, making a sticky mess. Someone wrote to the magazine and said that if you placed the small end of the cob in the hole of a tube pan and used an electric knife to slice the kernels off, the corn would fall into the cake pan, minus the mess. Sure enough, it worked like a charm. When the pan was full, all I had to do was fill Ziploc bags with the corn, flatten them out, and stack them in the freezer. I think freezing corn makes for a fresher-tasting product than canning, although I've done both.

I've found that slicing a small "x" on the end of a tomato before blanching makes the skin come off quicker, thus producing a more plump tomato for canning. Also I learned that tomatoes can be frozen whole and then diced into perfect pieces when semithawed and used in anything from soup to salsa. Whether you are a seasoned gardener or a rank amateur, there are always new and better ways of doing things, and it benefits everyone to pass them on. I am thankful the mountain people had enough time, patience, and inclination to teach an inexperienced young woman what they knew about preserving food. For me, it's become an all-consuming hobby, but I now realize that for them, it was survival.

Digging potatoes the old way: Lance and Olivia Thompson help Granddaddy dig potatoes.

When I moved here in 1980, and was just learning the ins and outs of how and when to plant a garden, my neighbor Johnny Coffey kept talking about planting by the signs. I had no idea what he was talking about until he pointed to his kitchen calendar (a Ramon's Brownie Calendar) and said, "No use planting the beans

Digging potatoes the new way! Jerry Lou and Dennis Hanger show 'em how it's done.

today, Son, it's a posey day." I still didn't have a clue but let it slide for fear he'd think me completely inept, which I was.

I got a firsthand lesson in planting by the signs when another neighbor asked to plant his green beans in a small section of earth in Johnny's garden. Johnny told him that Tuesday was the optimum day for getting the beans in the ground, and that's when we planted ours. The neighbor didn't come until three days later, and Johnny winked at me as he said, "His beans won't make . . . it's a posey day." The neighbor was ecstatic when in a month, his beans were blooming to beat the band. Ours looked a little peaked next to his, but when it came time to harvest, our rows were swelling with Tenderettes. To say his rows were skimpy was a vast

No matter how they're dug, potatoes bring smiles

A well-stocked pantry for the winter

understatement. He couldn't figure it out, but Johnny just gave me a nod and whispered, "Posey day."

I don't exactly know how planting by the signs works. But while growing up in Florida, I knew that the phases of the moon had a lot to do with the tides in the ocean, and certain human behaviors are influenced by the moon. For instance, any ER nurse will tell you that during a full moon, they see more people coming in with mental breakdowns, thus the terms lunacy and lunatic. Makes sense, but I don't know why.

Getting back to planting by the signs, any Ramon's Calendar or yearly *Farmer's Almanac* (which you can pick up at a Farm Bureau store) will give you the correct dates on which to do anything, from planting vegetables and cutting firewood to braiding your onions and worming your cattle. It's a pretty interesting process, at best. And for those wishing to keep the Sabbath holy, most "poor" planting days are on Sundays. Same goes for fishing, so there's no excuse for those skipping services to hit the lake!

Last year, we planted all our vegetables by the *Farmer's Almanac* and were amazed to find ourselves hauling out produce by the washtub full, while some of our neighbors complained they had planted their peas three times with little success. When they asked why they didn't get as good a crop, I gave Billy a sidelong glance and whispered, "Posey day!"

Hazel Fitzgerald; a Beech Grove favorite

25

Hazel Campbell Fitzgerald

Beech Grove, Virginia

One of the nicest parts of writing *Backroads* newspaper for twenty-five years was getting to meet the native people of the Blue Ridge Mountains. They are hearty, rugged folks who have lived by their wits and farmed the rocky land to survive. Although none of them had much in the way of material wealth, they were all rich in the things that really mattered. Hazel Campbell Fitzgerald is one of these people.

I first met Hazel when she called to ask if I'd be interested in having some old family photographs for the paper. I drove across the mountain to Beech Grove to see her and have been stopping by ever since. She is a quiet, unassuming woman with a warm personality and giving nature. When I married my husband, Billy, I became part of Hazel's family, since the branches of our family trees are intertwined. I was proud to publish her personal history in the pages of *Backroads* newspaper and even prouder to include them in this book, because she is truly one of the dear "Faces of Appalachia."

After Rufus Campbell and Liza Coffey married in 1918, Hazel was one of seven daughters and one son born to the couple. Hazel's grandparents on her mother's side were Henry and Millie Coffey and on her father's side, Charlie and Lou Campbell. Liza grew up in Chicken Holler. Her family was of the Dunkard faith, and they attended the Dunkard Church located at Love. Rufus's family lived on what is now the Hatter property, just down the mountain a few miles. The Campbells were strict Mennonites and probably attended Mountain View Church at the bottom of the hill.

Hazel's grandparents on her mother's side, Henry and Millie Coffey

Hazel's parents, Rufus and Liza Campbell

When Rufus and Liza married, they lived with his family for a while in a house that eventually burned down. It was located near the Frank Hatter home. From there, they moved up the mountain to a home belonging to Cyrus Coffey.

The first three daughters—Edith, Rachel, and Hazel—were born in the Love community. But when Hazel was two years old, the Campbells loaded all their possessions on an old horse-drawn spring wagon and moved east across the mountain to Hat Creek. It was so steep where their new house was located that everything had to be taken out of the wagon, put on a ground sled, and pulled the rest of the way by mule. Hazel said about the sheer steepness that they never could drive an automobile up to the house and had to walk in and out by foot.

The house, which Hazel called a "shanty," was one of seven or eight three-room residences that once housed railroad workers. The Bee Tree Railroad transported timber out of the mountains down to Massies Mill in the early years. But by the time the Campbell family moved to Nelson County, the train was no longer in operation, although the train track was still in place. Hazel said that she and her family walked the track many a day for a little entertainment.

Her father was a farmer by trade and worked for a man by the name of Clive Carter, who owned a great tract of land in that area. Rufus and Liza helped pick and sort apples in the fall and also cleared land or anything else that Mr. Carter wanted done. For their labor, they received free housing and got to keep everything they raised for their growing family's needs.

Juanita, Herman, Evelyn, and Vivian were born while the family lived in the shanty home. Barbara, the last child born to the Campbells, came after they had bought a six-room home in 1946. Barbara was the only child that had a doctor in attendance at birth. Hazel said a Dr. Dickie from Massies Mill came to deliver her youngest sister.

I asked Hazel if she could remember any of her early neighbors along Hat Creek, and names like Mrs. Robert Hampton, Mrs. Tice, and Dave and Eunice Grove came to her mind. Hazel laughed and said that she was always getting into some kind of foolishness with the Grove's son, Paige. She recalled one of their elementary school teachers at the Hat Creek School, a Lucy Harvey, whom she said was "right tight on us." For pure orneriness, she and Paige would go out at recess and eat wild onions so their breath would be bad for the rest of the day. For punishment, they had to stand in the corner by the woodstove. When the teacher wasn't looking, the children would reach their hands around the stovepipe, touch their fingers together, and giggle. As the Campbell children got older, they attended the Bryant School, then finished up at Fleetwood.

The family attended Jonesboro Baptist Church, which at that time sent a bus around the various small mountain hamlets to pick up the children.

Although it was all the Campbells could do just to feed and clothe their eight children, Hazel said they had such a good life together. Here she relates a little of what their life was like in the early years.

My dad raised all his own wheat and corn and would sack it up and put it on the wagon and take it to the mill in Massies Mill to be ground into flour and cornmeal for the winter. We had no newspaper or radio, so we didn't hear about all this shooting and killing like there is today. Folks seemed to get along much better back then; probably because we depended on each other more. We didn't have a lot of spare money, but our family had a lot of love, plenty of food on the table, and strong moral values. We respected our parents and other adults. We raised all of our own food, either from the garden or the animals we kept. We always had hogs [and] chickens, and Daddy killed a beef once a year. Mama raised turkeys to sell, and we picked all kinds of berries up in the mountains during the summertime.

I remember one time, right before Thanksgiving, Mama had raised this big fat turkey, and I kept hoping he'd break his leg so we could keep him for our own dinner instead of selling him. He was roosting in a tree and Daddy climbed up there to get him while my sister put a straw tick mattress under the tree just in case the turkey fell. They did manage to get him down, and he was sold, but I kept hoping he'd break his leg!

We had no indoor plumbing at all, and we had to carry water a long ways from the spring to the house. We had a springbox to keep our milk and butter cool. A typical breakfast for us back then would have been fried apples, meat, gravy, bread, and plenty of eggs. Seems like everything tasted so much better back then. We ate good because we worked hard. Working hard was a way of life. More than once, I've gone to the garden with Mama at nine o'clock at night to pick something for the next day's dinner.

All us kids helped hoe the corn and do the chores. Mama cooked on a wood cook stove in a separate outside kitchen, and we heated the house with wood. In the summer, we'd make a deep pond in the creek and take our baths there. In the winter months, we'd have to heat water and take a bath inside in a washtub. Mama used to wash our clothes in that washtub and would use bluing and lye soap to get the clothes real white. Mama did a lot of quilting, and that's where I learned my favorite hobby today. I figure I've made hundreds of quilts in my lifetime. I've made them for all my family and friends. It's what I love to do the best.

At Christmastime, we'd put up a tree and we'd string popcorn and paper chains to decorate it. Sometimes we'd take the silver paper from cigarette packs and wrap it around sycamore balls and hang them on the tree, too. Mama and Daddy would go down to Tommy Carter's store and buy each of us kids a little toy of some kind. Us girls usually got a doll baby, but I remember once I got a little wind-up tin toy where a dog chased a cat and the cat chased a fish. I don't know whatever happened to that toy, but I wish I would have hung on to it.

I met my husband, Clinie Fitzgerald, when I was around twenty-one years old. We never went out alone when we were dating; it just wasn't allowed back then. Mostly, he came over to my house and we talked together. At nine o'clock, my dad would announce it was "bedtime" and Clinie had better be getting up and going home. He used to date my sister Edith, but that didn't work out. I guess we *did,* and after courting for about a year, we married in September of 1943. He was a farmer, but when we married, he went to work at the Stanley Furniture Factory in Waynesboro. We stayed with Clinie's brother until we could get a house of our own. In 1960, we moved into our little house at Beech Grove. We had a happy life and always got along so good together. We had a son, Jesse, and a daughter, Carolina. But in 1966, Clinie passed away at only fifty-seven years of age. Jesse married Becky Sprouse, and they moved to Crimora, where they built a house several years ago. They have two children, Jesse, Jr., and Melinda Sue. Carolina married Charles Whitesell, and they are very happy together. Two years ago, I moved to Crimora, right next to Jesse and his family, and I'm pretty happy here.

Hazel has led a rich life, full of the joys and sorrows that come to us all, but she is happy and one of the most contented people I know. While we talked, there were so many humorous stories she told that I'd like to include a few before we close.

One was about her mother while she was still courting Rufus. One night, she was sleepwalking and came downstairs and wrapped her arms tightly around what she thought was her sweetheart, but turned out to be the stovepipe

An early photo of Hazel and Clinie

in the living room. She got her arms burned and was teased about it for the rest of her life. Or there was the time that Hazel and her sister Edith were sent out to churn butter. There was company coming and to try to hurry the churning process along, Hazel dumped some baking soda into the milk and ended up ruining the whole batch. The funniest story was about an old man named Herbert Harris, who worked for Hazel's dad. Rufus had to go somewhere, and told Herbert to stay and help Liza and the girls hoe the corn. Herbert was working in the garden, just below the women, when Liza dug into a yellow jacket's nest. She threw her hoe into the air and screamed and ran down the hill with her daughters. Herbert thought they were coming after him for some reason, and he commenced to running out ahead of them screaming, "I ain't done nothing . . . I ain't done nothing . . . don't hit me, *please* don't hit me!"

After we got done laughing, I thanked Hazel for a very entertaining afternoon, as well as for all the kindnesses she'd shown me down through the years. For example, one morning when she was still living in Beech Grove, she called to tell me to stop by her

Hazel showing off one of her "bow tie" quilts

house on the way home from delivering *Backroads* newspapers. I always brought Hazel a newspaper, and when I handed it to her that day, she handed me something back—a beautiful navy-blue and white quilt in her favorite "bow tie" pattern. It graces my bed today, and each time I pull its comforting warmth around me, I think of Hazel and what a warm and comforting friend she turned out to be.

Taken from the March 1995 *Backroads*

"Junior" Hatter at the Montebello Post Office

26

Alonzo L. "Junior" Hatter

Mountain Mail Carrier

One of my favorite people I've met since moving here is Alonzo L. Hatter, or "Junior" as he is known by everyone. Junior and his wife, Margie Coffey Hatter, own and operate Hatter's Goodwill Grocery, which is located on Route 56 in Tyro, Virginia.

In addition to being a familiar face at his store, he has also been the rural route carrier since 1962 when he began substituting for the regular carrier. When the man passed away, Junior was next in line, and he has been delivering the mountain people's mail ever since. In later years, he subcontracted the route to Darlene Fitzgerald, and now Junior only carries the mail when she is sick or, he says with a laugh, "When I feel like it!"

When I asked to interview him about what he does, I got a real treat when he invited me to ride along on his route so he could *show* me firsthand what he does.

On March 27, I accompanied Junior on the first leg of his daily route, which included the Montebello, Fork Mountain, and White Rock areas. Since these just happened to be three of my favorite places, I knew I was in for an enjoyable day.

As we bumped along Route 56 heading for Crabtree Falls, Junior put me right to work stuffing the day's mail in the black rural boxes along the way. His old red Jeep truck was the perfect vehicle to traverse the steep, curving mountain roads. On this beautiful spring day, you could drive most any car on the road, but in the icy winter months, a four-wheel-drive vehicle becomes a necessity.

Junior showed me where he was born and raised along the Tye River and told me more about this particular mail route. He said that he first has to drive to the Roseland Post Office to pick up, stack, separate, tie, and band the day's mail. He leaves Roseland and heads for the post office in Massies Mill to drop off sacks of mail there. He then swings around Route 680 by Flippin-Seaman Orchard, coming back to Route 56 about two miles below Tyro. He then crosses the river for about a mile and picks up mail at the Tyro Post Office. He drives up Harper's Creek as far as Tommy Fitzgerald's orchard, turns around, and heads for Coxes Creek and ends up at B. B. and Doris Hockaday's house, which is the last residence up Campbell's Mountain Road. After turning around, he hits Route 56 and drives to Montebello, delivering mail all the way. At the Montebello Post Office, he picks up the mail for White Rock. I met Joe Seaman, the Montebello postmaster, and he was good enough to come outside and pose for a picture with Junior under the Montebello Post Office sign.

Postmaster Joe Seaman and Junior

Then it's up the Fork Mountain Road and down the long, winding road toward White Rock. Junior said that this is the most remote part of the route. I looked at the different names on the mailboxes: Seaman, Mays, Painter, Bryant, and Fitzgerald. The same family names from generations before.

Coltsfoot, the earliest spring flower that blooms in the mountains, lined the dusty road and a trace of snow could still be seen clinging to the west side of the mountain. Last year's onions were hanging off someone's porch, still braided together and ready for the frying pan. I saw an old building that I like, and I asked Junior to stop so I could snap a picture. When I came back to the Jeep, he told me that was the old Fork Mountain School. "I think a lady by the name of Miss Cage taught there last," Junior informed me. He said that the school is now on Melvin Bryant's land.

Another unpainted wooden building fascinated me; it had green shutters and half-moon cutouts on the sides. "That's Pogue Chapel," said Junior. "Preacher Pogue helped start the little church, and he boarded with a man named Jeff Fitzgerald, who lived on the other side of Montebello."

As we rolled down the gravel road, I savored the living history lesson Junior was teaching me along the way. At last we came to the end of the road where there were no more houses and had to turn around. Junior said he sees a lot of wildlife on Fork Mountain. "Once I saw a little bear cub running along here. Another time I saw a wildcat, or a bobcat, they call 'em, up on the bank to my left, and he made one huge jump to the middle of the road and was gone. He looked straight ahead the whole time he was jumping . . . never did look around."

Next, Junior pointed out an old homeplace to me. "There's where Frank Bryant raised all of his children. And over there was Will Campbell's home. 'Square Will' they called him."

I asked Junior where Will got his unique nickname. I figured maybe he was a bit on the backward side or real shy. It was at this point that I realized there was a generation gap between Junior and I. For he went on to explain that Will Campbell was a magistrate for the area and could be counted on to be square (honest) in his dealings.

We drove up the Fish Hatchery road, where about six people live, and then back to Route 56 and onward to White Rock. Junior explained where the old post office used to be located. He said that for many years, the Anderson Grocery housed the government office. He delivered there for the last time sometime in the 1980s. Then the government office was moved over to Grant's Store. After around 1985, a new building was erected, and that's where it is to this day. Junior said that years back, the post office for the area was located at the confluence of the North Fork and the South Fork of the Tye River at Nash.

Down, down, down we drove, deeper and deeper into the mountain, until the familiar bridge of White Rock appeared. Here the gorge between the two mountains becomes so steep that I shuddered to think that Junior had to drive it during the icy winter months. They don't plow the road on a regular basis, so Junior would have to maneuver his Jeep the best he could. Even so, he only missed two days last winter because of deep snow.

"Now the '69 Flood, that was *really* something! There was no mail delivered for over a month because of road damage," Junior explained.

I asked what the worst part of his job was, and "bad roads" and "bad weather" came in tied for first place. And the best part? "Payday!" wailed Junior with his signature laugh. Somehow, I'm not convinced that is really the best part for this outgoing, gentle man.

Passing Durham's Run, Junior pointed out where an old sawmill run by Saylor Allen used to stand. Up the hollow is Raymond Allen's camp, where I've been many times for family reunions. We drove slowly by an innocent-looking spring trickling down the left side of the mountain. Junior said it's called the Clearing Branch. Immediately the hackles on my neck rose up. Creepy memories about a "haint" (ghostlike creature) that hung out by this particular spring came rushing back. Johnny Coffey told me stories about a "black shadowy thing" that would follow people when they passed the old spring, scaring the daylights out of them. I told Junior to step on it and us get out of there.

The Clearing Branch where the "haint" lives

We made the hairpin curve by the White Rock Schoolhouse and crossed over the wooden bridge spanning the Tye River that leads to Hercy and Burgess Coffey's homeplace. This is one of my all-time favorite places in White Rock. It also happens to be the home of Junior's wife's parents. Along with Hercy's house is his old mill, where people came to have their corn ground, and his father, Eli's, log cabin.

Junior said wistfully, "Forty-five years ago I carried Margie away from up here. But we didn't go far . . . just down to Tyro." They are still there and have run the Hatter's Goodwill Grocery for more than forty-one years. Junior's daddy, Alonzo Hatter, Sr., ran a store there before him, so I guess storekeeping runs in the family.

When we approached the little white house where Annie Carr lived, Junior told me to take the box of groceries in the back of the Jeep to her door and to bring back the money she'd hand me. Not knowing what was going on, I did what I was told. Sure enough, Annie came out on the porch and instructed me to carry the box to her kitchen table, then handed me some cash. I said thank you and went back to the Jeep. Junior explained that Annie had called in her grocery list to Margie earlier that morning, and Junior was the delivery man! As I was leaving, Annie told me not to forget to look in her mailbox. As I opened the door to the U.S.

postal box, there was a pint Mason jar full of sugar; a note was attached: "Please take this down to Lena's house; she's baking a cake and needs a little sugar."

We came to Lena Zirkle's house, and when I opened her mailbox to put in the mail, there was twenty-two cents inside a Mason jar lid. I handed Junior the money; he gave me a stamp and told me to lick it and put it on her outgoing letter. For some reason, just seeing that old zinc lid in the mailbox struck me funny, although it is a pretty handy way to keep change from rolling around. Lena poked her head out the door and asked if I'd brought the sugar from Annie for her cake, so I jumped out and made another delivery.

When, at last, we were going down the road, I said to Junior, "I thought putting something other than mail into government boxes was illegal. Does the postal service know that you do this?"

Junior replied, "Lynn, they don't even know where we *are*, so we kind of do what we want." Sounded like a good plan to me.

As we passed Preacher Billy Morris's house, a wave of loneliness tugged at my heart. He was such a part of the community that it seems impossible that he died and no longer lives here. He loved the old Mitchell Fitzgerald homeplace where he lived and Wildcat Creek that flowed to the side of the property. Seems I'll look over and see him working in the garden or rocking on the front porch taking in the view of Squaremouth Rocks high on the mountain above him. I don't think I'll ever pass by without feeling homesick for him.

Finally, we rounded the bend at Ralph Coffey's house, passed by Evergreen Christian Church, and headed back to Tyro, where we stopped at Junior and Margie's for a cup of coffee and a chat before he slipped out to deliver the rest of the mail. As I plopped down in one of Margie's overstuffed chairs and sipped my hot coffee, I could only smile and thank God that I've been so blessed to know wonderful folks like the Hatters.

As I drove back up the mountain toward Love, I thought about the day's events. I have to admit that the very best part of writing *Backroads* newspaper is having the opportunity to do all the odd

The Hatters at their store in Tyro

and assorted things that really interest me. Whether it's flying in a vintage airplane for a bird's-eye view of the mountains or riding in Junior Hatter's old red Jeep to deliver rural mail, I sure have a lot of fun doing my job!

Taken from the July 1987 *Backroads*

Outdoor privy at a farm in Beech Grove

27

Outdoor Privies

My introduction to outdoor privies came when I was a young girl visiting my Uncle Bob and Aunt Katie Wiltrout's rustic cottage on the shores of Lake Erie. The cottage had no indoor plumbing at the time, so we had to use the wooden facility located to the rear of the property up a well-worn path. I found it strangely freeing to sit quietly while the birds and crickets chirped around me. My older brother always ruined my last excursion before bedtime by whispering, "Don't let the bears get you!"

Many years later, when we started coming to the mountains for the weekends, I introduced my own young daughter to the quiet solitude of a "two-holer" at the hunting camp where we stayed. I remember the morning we were sitting side by side in the privy, and I gave instructions to "remember to flush" as I exited the wooden structure. Standing outside trying not to laugh, she emerged a few minutes later sheepishly announcing, "I couldn't find the flusher."

We ended up renting the same camp when we finally moved here in 1980, but by then the water had been turned on and we had the convenience of an indoor bathroom. We continued to make use of the old privy, however, when the electricity went off, which was often in the Blue Ridge Mountains where we lived. Gracing one wall of the camp's modern bathroom was a painting

I purchased by Waynesboro artist Joan Hinerman. The picture shows an outhouse with a light in the window and a television antenna on the roof. The title? *Affluence.* I had hung it in every bathroom of the homes I'd lived in until, alas, I lost it in a 1986 house fire.

Privy at the Weaver Camp in Chicken Holler   Privy at the Allen Camp up Durham's Run

Since the early years of the camp, although we've upgraded to indoor plumbing, I am still on the lookout for those distinctive wooden buildings located to the rear of older homes. It's surprising how many are still in existence and probably still being used for their intended purpose, especially at weekend camps in the mountains where people come to rough it.

Some privies—also called outhouses, Johnny houses, or outdoor toilets—are basic in structure, having one opening on which to sit. Others can accommodate two, three, and even four bottoms at a time, especially those belonging to families with many children. I remember Burgess Coffey telling me that her father had built a privy with different size holes for the various ages of his children:

small openings for the little ones, medium holes for the older children, and several larger ones for the adults.

And every household was equipped with a chamber pot or two, also known as a "Thunder Mug" or "Slop Jar." These portable potties were made of enamel or stoneware and were kept under the bed for use in times of emergency, sickness, inclement weather, or at night when a trek down the well-worn path was not desired. But it was understood that whoever used the chamber pot, emptied and cleaned it as well.

By far the grandest privy I've ever frequented is located in Coffeytown on the Macedonia Church property. The outside of the building is well maintained, but it's the *inside* that captures your attention. With electricity, a ceramic-tile floor, pictures gracing the walls, and a small basket of toiletries such as hand sanitizer and lotions, the double outhouse (his and hers) is a marvel to behold. And best of all, there are no spiders or creepy-crawlies to be seen anywhere!

The dictionary defines a privy or outhouse as a type of toilet in a small structure separate from the main building that does not have a flush and is not attached to a sewer. The building itself was usually constructed of wooden boards, but some built more permanent ones of brick or natural stone to compliment a home made from the same materials. Privies were situated over an excavation hole from three to six feet deep, and a bucket filled with lime was often placed on the floor within reach so a scoop could be thrown down the hole as needed to reduce odors. Ventilator pipes that resembled a smokestack rose from seat level and extended out the roof to help cut down on methane gas buildup.

We associate a "moon" cut into a privy door as kind of a standard ornamentation on these buildings. I always assumed it was simply to let in sunlight or air, but while researching the topic, I found out that these vents often doubled as symbols for gender identification. The crescent shape was the universal symbol of womankind. Thus a moon, sawed into a privy door, served to let folks know this was the "Ladies Room." In early times, a sunburst pattern was cut into the door of the men's privy, which indicated

Coffeytown's upscale dual privy, with electricity, tile floors, and a basket of hand products

Interior of the Coffeytown privy

"Old Sol," the sun. These symbols were necessary, since during Colonial times, only a small portion of the population could read or write. But I have also seen stars and diamond shapes cut into the doors.

Before the advent of paper products, folks relied on the standard Sears and Roebuck catalogs for taking care of personal hygiene inside the privy. The catalogs were thick and ripped-out pages would be available for a long time. Before that, country folks who had access to large gardens used the cobs from shelled corn for the task. For those not well acquainted with the texture of fresh shelled corn cobs and wince at the thought of scraping delicate flesh with husks associated with the term "rough as a cob," the old-timers say that fresh ones are soft to the touch. And since red cobs outnumbered white two to one, the trick was to use a red cob first, a white one next, and another red one if it was needed.

A unique Buick hood canopy over R. T. Toler's two-holer

The photos used for this chapter on privies were all taken within a short distance of our cabin in Love, Virginia, and the buildings continue to be used or are just allowed to stand as a nostalgic remembrance of yesteryear.

Over the years that *Backroads* newspaper was in print, I published a little story entitled "A Matter of Communication" several times because folks found it humorous and always asked for it. I am including it here for those who never got to read it.

A MATTER OF COMMUNICATION

There was a nice lady who was a little old fashioned. She was considering a week's vacation in sunny Florida at a particular campground, but she wanted to make sure of the accommodations first.

Uppermost in her mind were the toilet facilities, but she couldn't bring herself to write the word "toilet" in a letter. After careful deliberation she settled on "bathroom commode." But when she wrote that down, it still sounded a little too forward, so she rewrote the entire letter to the campground owner and referred to the "bathroom commode" as the "B.C."

"Does the campground have its own B.C.?" is what she actually wrote.

The owner was baffled by the euphemism, so he showed the letter around to several people staying at the campground, but they could not decipher it either. Finally, the owner concluded that she must have been referring to the local Baptist church so he sat down to respond. . . .

> Dear Madam,
>
> I regret very much the delay in answering your letter, but now I take pleasure in informing you that a "B.C." is located nine miles north of the campground, and is capable of seating 250 people at one time. I admit that it is quite a distance away if you are in the habit of going regularly, but no doubt you will be pleased to know that a great number of people take their lunches along and make a full day of it. They arrive early and stay late!
>
> The last time my wife and I went was six years ago, and it was so crowded that we had to stand up the entire time we were there. It may interest you to know that right now, there is a benefit supper planned to help raise money to buy more seats. The supper is going to be held in the basement of the B.C.
>
> I would like to say that it pains me very much not to be able

to go more regularly, but it is surely from no lack of desire on my part. As we grow older, it seems to be more of an effort, particularly in cold weather.

If you do decide to come down and stay at our campground, perhaps I could go with you to the B.C. the first time; sit with you and introduce you to all the other folks who go there. Remember . . . we are widely known as a friendly community, so come on down and we'll all enjoy the B.C. together!

Homer and Louise at their farm in Montebello

28

Homer and Louise Anderson

Montebello, Virginia

I'm not sure of the exact date I met Homer and Louise Anderson, but I knew them well enough to videotape their wedding in 1988 and to be part of that memorable celebration along with their family and longtime friends. So it was with much pleasure that I was able to talk to them both about being born and raised in the mountain hamlet of Montebello and find out more about their early lives growing up there.

Both Andersons know firsthand what being a general merchandise merchant was all about, since Louise's parents owned and operated Farris's Store, a stone's throw away from where they now live. Homer's first wife was Pauline Robertson. Her family ran a store where Homer worked and retired from in 1981. A lot of things have changed since they were children, and Backroads readers will now get a glimpse of what life was like in the days of their youth.

Louise was born on January 27, 1922, one of fourteen children—ten of whom survived—born to Albert and Ollie Fitzgerald Farris. Albert was an immigrant from Syria who had come to the United States in 1910. He began as a peddler, going door to door selling all types of merchandise. From that humble beginning, Albert carved out a niche for himself and opened a general store that became very familiar to all those living near Montebello. Louise remembers her mother and most of her siblings helping in the business, waiting on customers and delivering goods to nearly everyone in the community. One side of the country store contained groceries, the other, dry goods such as shoes and hardware. The Farris homeplace still stands on the steep hill just outside the village itself.

The area where the Farris Store was located was called Statonsville back then, named after a local family. What Louise remembers most about growing up were the people. "This mountain was just full of people," she recalls. "Bob Booth was the community farrier, and Beauregard Harvey made coffins when someone died. There was a large cannery that was run by R. D. Allen, where folks could preserve their garden produce in tin cans. My grandparents, Wade and Nelly Fitzgerald, ran a grist mill at the site of our present home, where they ground cornmeal and buckwheat flour. My grandfather was also the village blacksmith at the time.

"We had four churches near our home: Mount Paran Baptist Church, where I have been a member since I joined and was baptized at fourteen years of age; a small Dunkard church; South Mountain Chapel; and Pogue's Chapel out on Fork Mountain. There were one-room schoolhouses at Norval's Flat and Fork Mountain, but most of us kids went to the four-room Montebello School, which had eight grades. Both of our families used to board a lot of the teachers who taught there."

Homer and Louise were sweethearts during their teen years, but they ended up marrying different people. Louise, at age seventeen, eloped to Reedsville, North Carolina, with Everett Campbell, whose family lived in the Beech Grove community. The couple lived with his family for seven years before moving into their own home in the Rockfish Valley. The Campbell's had three children, Everett, Bruce, and Shirley, and when they were grown, Louise went to work at the Del Monte Frozen Foods Corporation, from which she later retired. Her husband passed away in 1972, and until 1988, Louise continued to live at their Rockfish Valley home. Then she made a special move back to Montebello, but we'll talk about that later.

Homer was born on October 22, 1915, the only son of Jacob Yost and Lottie Catherine Hite Anderson. His sister, Hettie, came fifteen months later. Before he was born, Homer's parents lived out on Fork Mountain, but when Lottie was due with her son, the couple moved in with her parents, who at that time lived up the hollow from Aubrey Bradley's home. Later the Andersons built a home close to the Hites.

After Homer's grandfather Alfred died, his grandmother Lula Haney Hite married Henry Painter, and Jacob moved his family to a farmhouse closer to the Painters to help Henry with the farming. Homer was eight years old when they moved to what he refers to as his homeplace. Although his father was primarily a farmer, he was also the community barber and set up shop, complete with a barber chair, in back of the grocery store that Homer would later buy. Homer said he never paid for a haircut until after his father died. He remembers how all the young men would come on Saturday afternoons to get their hair cut for a dollar.

Homer wistfully recalls how back then, everyone made time to visit one another, especially during the holidays. From the first of December to the end of January, people would make the rounds and visit every person in the Montebello area. He remembers going to Louise's parent's house and eating his first cabbage rolls, which he thought "were the best things I had ever tasted!" The Farris family also had one of the first radios, and folks would congregate on Saturday nights to listen to the Grand Ole Opry while eating cookies and cider that Ollie Farris had prepared. Or perhaps they'd have an autumn wood chopping, during which the men would cut firewood all day and have a dance later that night. They would go over to Aubrey Layton's home, who lived where the current firehouse is now located, and move all his furniture out in the yard so they could have a big, empty room to dance in. The musicians would stand in the corner to play while someone would do the calling for the Virginia Reel or a square dance. Carl and Lonnie Ramsey would play guitars along with Johnny Floyd and Downy Snead who played fiddles. Homer's dad, Jacob, whom he said always believed in having a good time, played the banjo so well that he won the prize of a five-dollar gold piece in a music contest over in Shipman.

Along with the seemingly endless amount of physical work that a farm entails, young people also had their fun. There were apple butter boilings, corn shuckings, picnics on Spy Rock, and fishing for native trout in the deep pools at Crabtree Falls. Homer tells of the time he and his father contracted a load of extract wood for Louise's parents, and with his share of the money, Homer bought a pair of sixteen-inch high-top boots, a .22 rifle, and a pair of riding breeches. "Now you talk about one sassy dude . . . that was me in them riding pants," laughs Homer.

Like many young men, Homer lived at home until he married. When he and Pauline Robertson tied the knot on August 1, 1936, he was already working in her father's grocery store. For years, Pauline's father was the postmaster of Montebello, sorting mail in Beauregard Harvey's old coffin house. When the Bradley family, who at the time owned the grocery, decided to sell out, the Robertsons bought the store and incorporated the post office inside. After marriage, the couple lived with Pauline's family for a few years before getting a place of their own. Later, they tore down the old cannery and built a large brick home on the site. The Andersons had two sons, Steve and Timothy.

The old Anderson's Grocery in Montebello

Homer continued to work in the store, and after Mr. Robertson's health failed, he bought the business in 1951 and renamed it Anderson's Grocery. He remembers people coming in to buy their winter supplies, one-hundred-pound bags of pinto and cranberry beans and a hundred pounds each of flour and cornmeal. The average cost for staples for a family for the entire winter was under twenty dollars.

There was a long bench in front of a big pot-bellied woodstove, and on days when the weather was bad, men would congregate on the bench to swap stories. The "regulars" were Frank Humphreys, Taylor Whitesell, Pomp and Willis Layton, John Fitzgerald, Aubrey Bradley, and John Campbell, to name a few. Homer laughs out loud, saying, "If that bench could talk, it could make me a millionaire today. You never heard such tales in your life! These men killed bears so big that they couldn't drag them out of the woods with a tractor. And they caught fish so big they had to erect derricks to lift them out of the water."

Homer closed the doors to Anderson's Grocery and retired in 1981. He says he misses it to this day, and it was the people who made him love his work.

Pauline's health gradually failed, and she passed away in June 1988. In August of that year, a ninetieth birthday party was being planned for Louise's mother at Coyner Springs Park, and Louise asked her mother if there was anybody from Montebello that she would like to invite. When Ollie mentioned her fondness for Homer, who was now alone, Louise didn't want to call and invite him, for the simple reason that she thought he might think she was after him in some way. What she didn't know was that Homer wasn't even aware that Louise had been a widow for sixteen years. She tried getting her sisters to call, but they encouraged her to be the one to talk to him. At the same time, Homer was mourning the loss of Pauline so acutely that he remembers sitting at his table saying, "Lord, if this is all you've got left for me, then I wish you'd just take me home." Louise made the call and Homer accepted. When he arrived at the birthday party, Homer went straight to Louise to say hello, and put his arm around her. "That was it," said

Homer. Right then, they both knew that their earlier teenage romance would somehow be rekindled and that they would marry and spend the rest of their lives together.

I remember the wedding well. October 29, 1988, was a beautiful fall day on which to be married. After a three-month courtship, the beaming couple exchanged vows at Mount Paran Baptist Church in a celebration that included their whole family. Homer was smiling from ear to ear, handsome in his white tuxedo and not looking his age of seventy-three. Louise was dressed in the most beautiful vintage-looking wedding dress I've ever seen and, like her bridegroom, all smiles. Homer says, "I never had as much fun in my life at I did at our wedding." Louise adds, "I feel that the good Lord brought us together, and we've had a wonderful ten years."

Homer and Louise pose for a wedding portrait

After a honeymoon at Peaks of Otter, the Andersons came back to Montebello to live in the brick home that Homer had built many years before. They did everything together, right from the start, including cutting firewood, putting up fences, and feeding the cows. Louise laughs and says she's the "gate opener" when Homer cranks up his tractor and goes out to feed. Recently celebrating their tenth anniversary, the Andersons reflect on the

Homer and Louise on their wedding day

irony of marrying and being so happy after all the years in between. Homer sums it all up with a smile and a twinkle in his eyes: "We've had a wonderful ten years, sure enough!"

Taken from the January 1999 *Backroads*

The Andersons inside the old store

As of this writing on March 21, 2011, Homer and Louise Anderson will be celebrating their twenty-third wedding anniversary this coming October. They still reside in the same home near the village of Montebello and continue to do things, as always, together.

Homer out with his cattle

Ora Robertson at her daughter's home in Stuarts Draft

29

Ora Campbell Robertson

Stuarts Draft, Virginia

It was years ago when I first saw the woman working in her garden. She had that peaceful, unhurried look that many of the older people possess, and I always wished I could get up my nerve to stop and ask if she'd let me take her picture. Dressed in her faded wash dress, old-fashioned apron, and straw hat, she was the perfect candidate for the pages of *Backroads*. But the road to "Thacker's Flats" was busy and so was I, and the visit never transpired. I'd always regretted that I hadn't found the time to meet this interesting-looking woman.

Time went by, and a sweet lady by the name of Agnes Thacker wrote to me about renewing her subscription to the newspaper. In the letter, she mentioned that her mother, Ora Campbell Robertson, was raised in the Love area and was still very active for her ninety years. Later that evening, I called Agnes to ask if I could perhaps interview her mother for the February 1992 issue of *Backroads*. It was then that I realized the lady I was to interview was the same woman I had long admired on the way to Stuarts Draft.

The day I went to talk to her, I was dressed in my customary Levi's and sweatshirt. I started laughing and knew it would be a great visit when Ora's daughter, Agnes, announced, "See, Mama, I *told* you Lynn wasn't prissy!"

Ora had said that she wasn't about to change her clothes for someone she didn't know, because she had to go out and feed her chickens afterward. It sure broke the ice, and we all went inside the house to talk.

I found Ora to be one determined, tough-minded woman. A person who could hold her own with anyone yet had an ever-present smile on her face. I had never met anyone her age so full of themselves. I decided right there that meeting Ora was worth the wait, and I vowed to come back later in the summer and take that long-sought-after picture of her in the garden.

Ora came into this world on April 13, 1901, one of six children born to William Franklin and Louetta Campbell. Their homeplace was high on a flat ridge across from the present entrance to Sherando Lake on Route 664. Ora had two brothers: Fred (who died of diphtheria at seven years of age) and Roy; and three sisters, Madge, Minnie, and Daisy. She is now the last-surviving member of her immediate family.

Ora's parents, Frank and Louetta Campbell

When Ora was just a tiny child, her parents separated; her mother took two of the children and went to live at her Aunt Sally Lowery's house near Stuarts Draft. She then rented a small cabin from Dr. Dodge that was located on Gertie's Lane, just down the road from Sally.

Ora was perhaps two years old when her mama left, and although her father hired a black woman named Lou Hamilton to help with her care, it didn't seem to work out very well. Ora was too small to help in their fields, and Frank couldn't watch her, so he asked a neighboring family if they would keep her. The Bridge family lived only a short distance through the woods, and Ora was very happy living there. Bettie Bridge, mother of Junie and grand-mother of Jesse, took good care of the little girl until she was seven years old. Ora remembers the day that drastically changed her life.

"I remember I was outside picking up small rocks and putting them into neat piles, because Junie told me for every pile I could make, he'd give me some candy. I was really looking forward to get-ting that candy when I noticed my older brother Roy coming across the field. He told Aunt Bettie that his father had sent him over to borrow some nails. Bettie went inside the house to get the nails, Roy sneaked up behind me, grabbed me up, and ran on home with me. My father had waited until I was big enough to watch the sheep and hoe the corn, and then sent Roy over to steal me back."

Jesse Bridge's family in 1907; Ora at bottom right next to the dog

When I asked Ora if the Bridge family ever came to see about her, she told me that her daddy had a mean temperament, and people were afraid to mess with him, so she ended up staying there and working for a year or more. When she was nine, Ora decided to run away and live with her mother. Ora and her two remaining sisters planned to just up and leave one day. They walked down through the mountains and cut through Sand Springs by the CCC Camp and made it to the Coal Road. They stopped at Kennedy Mines where Minnie's future husband Quincey worked. He took them up on a little hill and pointed out a path through the woods; he told the girls that the path would take them to their mother. They stayed on it and eventually found their way to her.

Ora recalls, "My father remarried a girl by the name of Pearl Nuchols, and they had three boys, Frank, Bill, and Ray, who were my half-brothers. Once, my father rode a horse over to where I was living and demanded that I come home with him and help with the work. He told me if I didn't climb up on his horse that he'd whip me with his riding stick until I did. I told him that he could keep on whipping me, but I was *not* going back with him. My mother caught wind of his being there, trying to take me back with him, and she came out with a shotgun and started shooting at him. He got the idea pretty quick and left.

Once, my sister-in-law May and I waited until dusky dark and went down to where the men parked the dinky train from Kennedy Mines each evening. We stole the lever car and pumped our way over to the store in Lipscomb and then back again. It's a wonder we didn't get killed jumping the track, but we never did."

Ora married John Robertson when she was sixteen years old. They ran off to Hagerstown, Maryland, on the passenger train that came through Stuarts Draft each afternoon at three o'clock. After they got all the way up there, they found out John was also underage and couldn't sign the marriage certificate, so he had to ride the train all the way back home, get his mother to sign for them, and then catch the afternoon train back to pick up Ora, who had stayed in a hotel while he was gone.

After the couple came back, they stayed with John's mother for a while before setting up housekeeping in their first house on Route 610, near Sherando. They moved a few times over the years but always stayed in the same vicinity, finally settling down in a house that John built just off Gertie's Lane near Shenandoah Acres Resort. They had a good life together. John worked at the Kennedy Mines, digging iron ore, and in the fall months, he picked apples and pruned the trees. Ora stayed home to raise their two children, Hobert Sylvester ("Buddy") and Agnes Mae. In the fall, Ora also went to work in the apple orchards to supplement their income. Ora loved going hunting with her husband who kept coon dogs. She has always enjoyed being outdoors and saw to it that their family cow was milked, the hogs were fed, and her chickens cared for.

John died in 1977, but Ora continued to live at their home with Agnes or other family members who stayed with her at night. Today she lives most times with Agnes, although she goes back and forth from Agnes's to her own home on Gertie's Lane. The garden, the chickens, and a cat named Sue are all kept at Agnes's house now.

Ora's son never married, but Agnes wed Floyd "Junior" Thacker and made their home along Route 610. In the 1940s, they opened a country gas and grocery store known as "Thacker's Flats." They had tall, glass-topped gas pumps and carried Phillips 66 gasoline. They ran the

Courtesy of Ora Robertson

Ora holding two raccoons that she shot

family-owned grocery until Junior had an accident at the blanket factory where he also worked and became ill. For a while he operated a small TV and radio repair shop, but eventually even that proved too much for him and he retired. The Thackers had four children: Delmer, their eldest son, whom they called "Doodle"; then came Bobby; a daughter Violet; and nine years later, baby Rosalee. The Thackers have always been a very happy family.

Sitting there with Agnes and Ora, sipping coffee and sharing memories, turned out to be such a nice afternoon. We laughed a lot at some of Ora's early shenanigans, and I found I really liked the spunky little woman sitting across from me. At one point, Agnes got up to retrieve her mother's harp (mouth organ), and Ora proceeded to play a couple of lively tunes for me. "Home Sweet Home," "Sally Get Your Hair Cut," and "Tell It to Jesus" never sounded better than on Ora Robertson's harp. We went outside to try to get a picture of her feeding her chickens, but my camera made them skittish, so I settled on a close-up of her smiling face.

During the interview, as Ora was talking, I thought to myself, "What a lucky girl I am to be able to come into a person's home I've never met, take their photograph, sit with them and record stories that have been passed down through the generations, and put them into a small mountain newspaper called *Backroads*." I am humbled by each person who allows me to come into their home and trusts me to write their family histories. It is satisfying work that I have come to love, and I thank those like Ora Campbell Robertson who make it all possible.

Taken from the February 1992 *Backroads*

Maxie and Mary Seaman; Montebello, Virginia

Don Snyder gathering buckets of maple sap to be boiled into syrup

30

Making Maple Syrup

Don Snyder; Hermitage, Virginia

A few years back, a man by the name of Don Snyder told me about a unique hobby he enjoys during the winter months. According to the county extension agent, Don is the only person in Augusta County participating in the old-time craft of tapping sugar maple trees and boiling down the sap into maple syrup. This is strictly a home-use operation, since he and his wife, Gladie, make only three to five gallons a year. They use the sweet syrup for themselves, as well as giving some to family and friends who enjoy the distinctive flavor. For those of us who were raised on the thick, store-bought pancake syrup, Mother Nature's brand is quite a change. Thinner, but more flavorful, the boiled-down sap from the maple trees is also much richer than the commercial varieties.

Don said he had his first experience with tapping maple trees when he was a boy back in northern Indiana. Each family had a little maple grove from which they made their own syrup each spring. His family was no exception, so over the years, he became familiar with the process.

When the Snyder's bought their present home thirty-eight years ago, most of the property was woods. They constructed a picnic facility at the edge of the woods near their home. About twenty-five years ago, Don was clearing out some brush around this area when he cut the end off a low-hanging maple limb. Immediately, the branch began to "bleed" or drip sap. "Although I knew our woods were filled with maples, that was the first time the possibility of making our own syrup ever occurred to me," said Don.

He went to Staunton and found a hardware store that carried syrup-making taps, and he bought all they had plus a dozen empty paint buckets. He came home and went to work, tapping a half dozen trees. When he had a couple of gallons of sugar water, he brought it into the house and began boiling it down on the kitchen stove. He said the first batch tasted great, and he knew he was in business!

A tapped sugar maple on Don Snyder's farm

By the next spring, Don had been unable to find any more taps, so he asked a local machine shop owner if he could fabricate some for him. In the end, the machinist did make the taps, but they weren't exactly like the ones that were bought at the hardware store. Nevertheless, they did the trick. Don bought more paint buckets but later on switched to plastic one-gallon jugs. These seemed to work better and kept the sap cleaner.

Don made another trip to the machinist to ask if he could make a container in which to boil down the sap. The man manufactured a thirty-five-gallon, stainless steel tank which fit into the fireplace at the Snyder's picnic area. Since there was a built-in wood supply on the property, Don began boiling down larger quantities of the sap outdoors instead of in the kitchen.

During the next several years, Don found more commercially manufactured taps and at present, he drives from 150 to 200 of the taps into fifty or sixty trees on his property. If the sap "runs" anywhere near normal, he makes three to five gallons of syrup from the liquid that is boiled down. It takes between fifty-five and sixty gallons of sugar water to make one gallon of syrup. Commercial syrup makers boil it down sixty-five to one.

Mother Nature herself 100 percent determines when, where, and how much the sap runs each year. The "run" starts as early as the end of January to as late as the middle of March. It depends entirely on temperatures and frozen and thawing ground. After the run starts, usually cold nights and warm days will keep the flow running. If it is warm for too long, the run will stop, as it will if it is continually cold.

The run may last only two days or up to ten days. The sap may run only once or as many as four different times. A tree that yields sap one year may not do so the next year. Sometimes sap can be extracted from only one side of the tree, usually the south side. And if rain gets into the sap, it will ruin the syrup's taste. One year, Don had to throw out a whole batch because rain got in it. Although Don says he knows the above facts are true, he's not sure *why* they are true.

According to Snyder's information, there are seventeen different

Maple syrup being boiled down

varieties of sugar maples in the United States, and only these types yield the sap that is used to make syrup. He was told by an authority on the subject that to identify a sugar maple, check the color of the leaves in the fall. If the leaves are red, yellow, or orange or any combination of the three colors, it's truly a sugar maple. A silver maple, for instance, is not a sugar maple.

The Snyders don't buy any syrup but use what they make until it is gone. Since Don has retired, this project is something to keep him busy in the slow months of the year; it is also a great conversation subject. He says it's amazing the number of folks who know little or nothing about this hobby and have never seen the actual operation in progress. He says he has never boiled the sap down far enough to make maple sugar; he is happy to just stick to syrup making.

Special thanks to Don Snyder of Hermitage for sharing his knowledge about syrup making here in Augusta County and for providing me with a sample of his product, which will go perfectly on some homemade buckwheat pancakes!

Taken from the April 1988 *Backroads*

"Pug" Allen playing one of his old–time fiddles

31

Luther Gorman "Pug" Allen

Stuarts Draft, Virginia

I t's called old-time mountain music, and to some it may sound a little ragged around the edges; but for the ones who were raised around it, it's literally music to their ears. Once a thriving sound in the hills of the Blue Ridge, genuine old-time music seems to be fading, like so many of the traditional customs of our area.

The instruments are the banjo, fiddle, and a few guitars, and this type of music differs from country/western and bluegrass in that there is not as much singing. It is a repetitious playing of old mountain standards, such as "Soldier's Joy," "Barbara Allen," and "Turkey in the Straw." These types of infectious, foot-stomping, hand-clapping tunes were what barn dances were famous for. It was the poor man's main source of entertainment after long hours of cutting timber and working in the garden and fields. Barn dances were where kids climbed up the ladder into the hayloft and watched as Mama traded her flour-dusted apron for a whirl around the floor on Papa's arm. The music transformed an ordinary barn into an evening of magic under the soft glow of coal-oil lamps hanging from the rafters. Shy, giggling girls waited patiently against the walls while favorite beaus mustered up the courage to ask for a dance.

The older folks who played for these dances are slowly passing away and, with them, their special music. We are fortunate to have in our area a man who still regularly plays the old songs in the old way. Luther Gorman Allen, or "Pug" as he's known to all, is one of these musicians who can play any tune you name. He is carrying on the rich tradition of the Scottish/Irish descendants who made their homes in the Blue Ridge Mountains well over a hundred years ago.

Born some eighty years ago over on the North prong of the Tye River near Durham's Run, Pug was one of eleven children who grew up in a music-oriented family. Back then, most folks could play some type of instrument, and making music was a way of life. Pug was ten or twelve years old when he first picked up a guitar and started learning to play it. He more or less taught himself, watching the older folks play and then imitating their particular style. By mimicking the way they played, without realizing it, the music became ingrained in him. After he had mastered guitar, he went on to the banjo and mandolin. About the mandolin, Pug says, "I sat up all night and never got nothin' out of it." He then tried the dobro, which was nothing more than an old flat top guitar, that he played with the back of an old Case knife he carried in his pocket.

Courtesy of George Allen

The Allen family; Pug at bottom left and his father, Andy, at top right

In 1920, Pug married Mattie Hatter from Montebello and went to work in timber, cutting extract wood (dead, standing chestnut).

He bought and sold large tracts of real estate and always made a job for himself so that he wouldn't have to work for anybody else. The young couple moved to Bedford for two years, then returned to a farm in Greenville. From there they moved to their present home in Stuarts Draft.

Pug continued to play music and soon became very well known in the music circles as one of the best. In 1948, he and several other family members were regulars on radio station WREL in Lexington, Virginia. The group was billed as The Skyline Boys and had an hour-

Mattie Hatter and Pug Allen on their wedding day

long slot every Saturday afternoon that was sponsored by the Fitzgerald Lumber Company of Buena Vista. They also played at other broadcasting stations in the Harrisonburg and Lynchburg areas.

When Pug was around forty years old, he decided he needed a change from the banjo so he decided to take up the fiddle. Pug's brother, Eugene "Hoot" Allen, was already an established fiddle player, and it didn't take long for Pug to follow suit; fiddle duets

(L–R) Agnes Thacker, Irene Allen, Eddie Dodd, and George and Pug Allen

became common in the Allen household. Johnny Coffey told me the most beautiful fiddle music he ever heard, that never failed to bring tears to his eyes, was played by Hoot's two sisters, Bess and Estelle, who played in harmony.

Pug has been buying, selling, and trading fiddles for around forty years, and he has quite a large collection. He has sold fiddles to every major musician in the country who is serious about learning

The Skyline Boys in 1948: (L—R) Neil Mace and Pug, Glenn, Hoot, and George Allen

the old style of playing. His present collection boasts maker's names such as Maggini, Joseph Canary, Paganini, and three or four Stradivarius copies. He handles them with tender care and plays them reverently. The oldest fiddle in his collection is dated 1634 and bears the name Maggini. I found it hard to believe something that old could still be in good condition, but Pug says, "The older a fiddle, the better the sound."

In 1979, Pug was invited to perform at the Festival of Traditional American Dance and Music in Massachusetts. The festival was sponsored by the Country Dance and Song Society of America and was held at the Pine Wood Camp. There, along with numerous other musicians who played the old-style music, Pug taught young people how to keep the flavor of traditional mountain music alive for future generations. He also played up to five and six dances a day so that people could learn the art of clogging, flat footing, and many other kinds of dances that are popular in our area. It was the highlight of a musically enriched life for Pug.

In addition to music, another big interest in Pug's life has been the rugged sport of bear hunting. He has been out in the woods since the first hunting season that his daddy plunked him down at thirteen years of age on a tree stand with a single-barrel shotgun. He recalls the very first bear he killed when he was twenty-five. "I killed it over on Spy Creek with a Winchester rifle. I threw it over my old horse and brought it out of the woods. I guess it weighed in at around two-hundred pounds." He also remembers the biggest bear that was ever taken, to his knowledge. "There were about five or six men in the hunt, and I had five dogs set out on the bear. Snow was about knee deep, and after a while, we had to tie up the horses and walk. We traced the bear over to the big DePriest Mountain in Nelson County, and the paw prints were so big that a man's hat would not even cover them. A man by the name of Herman Maddox finally killed the bear, and we estimated it weighed somewhere in the neighborhood of seven hundred pounds. The hide alone weighed in at nearly fifty pounds. There was six inches of fat over his whole body, and his old stomach nearly drug the ground when he walked." A smile at the memory creased Pug's face, then he picked up a banjo and started playing a lively rendition of "Red Wing."

The pleasant morning came to an end, after learning many new things about an old-time tradition worth preserving. Pug's gracious wife, Mattie, had prepared a dinner fit for a king and invited me to say and share the meal with them. Pug's son, Gorman, said grace, and then we passed around plates of spare ribs, turnips, snap beans, and hoecake. There was more talk about music as we sat around the table and I was glad to be there listening to the conversation. Another fine family and another fine tradition has passed my way, and I am thankful to have met and known folks like the Allens, who are worthy of life's richest blessings.

Taken from the March 1985 *Backroads*

Martha Mays at her Fork Mountain home

32

Martha Phillips Fitzgerald Mays

Montebello (Fork Mountain), Virginia

The first daughter of James Henry and Josie Elizabeth Phillips was born on her grandfather's birthday, so her parents bestowed his name on her, and she became Martha Edward Phillips until her wedding day.

Martha grew up with her sister, Dorothy, and brother, Austin, along the north prong of the Tye River across from Ida Sorrell's cabin near White Rock. Her father had bought the land and home from Pierce Allen, who was also responsible for building the White Rock School.

As children, Martha and her siblings worked "from the time we could," hoeing corn, milking cows, tending the garden, chopping wood, and feeding the many farm animals their family kept. But along with all the hard work came times of fun for the Phillips children when neighbors came to visit. While the grownups talked on the porch, the children played hide-and-seek or jump rope.

Church played a big part in Martha's life, and she can remember well the times they'd walk to Sunday services down at White Rock Christian Church and listen to the preacher, Riley Fitzgerald, deliver his sermons. Riley used to ride his horse from his home, which was located on the south fork of the Tye River, down to the church to preach at either the morning or evening service. Martha said she could still remember how people used to walk to the evening meetings by the light of homemade lanterns; pop bottles filled with kerosene with a twist of flannel for a wick.

She was baptized when a young girl at the "deep hole" in the Tye River, just below the old Massie Camp, and was cautioned by her father on the evils of sitting in the last row

Martha's sister, Dorothy, at the White Rock homeplace

of the church, saying, "Don't sit on the last pew, because that's where all the mischief starts!"

When it came time for her to start school, Martha attended the White Rock School, which was located right next to the church, and remembers her first teacher as being Sal Hatter.

Taught to cook by her mother when she was about eleven years old, Martha laughs and says, "I've been at it ever since."

The family washed their clothes outdoors in a boiling kettle of water and used homemade lye for bleaching the white articles. Once the clothes were properly washed and rinsed clean, they were hung over old telephone lines to dry, because the lines weren't prone to rust like regular wire was. If they ran out of room, the clothes were simply strung on the picket fence that surrounded the house.

Martha's father, James Henry Phillips, worked in timber, made shingles, and peeled tanbark, like so many of the mountain men. "He went to work by lantern light and came home by lantern light," laughed Martha softly. "He worked at the different saw mills around the area, John Zirkle's and Wheeler Fauber's."

Saturday evening lawn parties were held in the summertime to benefit the church. Ladies sold baked goods, such as cakes and cookies, and cold lemonade, which was made from icy spring water because they did not have ice during the hot summer months.

Christmas was a happy time in the Phillips home. Although

they did not receive many gifts, it was a time for love and visits from neighbors and relatives. Delicious baked goods, such as sweet cakes and molasses cookies flavored with ginger, were made and freely eaten.

Funerals were held at the White Rock Cemetery, and Martha remembers Marshall Fitzgerald being the song leader at the burials. "He always had the people sing 'Shall We Gather at the River' and 'Going Down the Valley One by One.'"

When Martha was thirteen years of age, her family moved to Norval's Flats near Painter Mountain. She lived there until she was twenty-four years old. At that time, she married Isaac Fitzgerald, and they lived with Martha's parents for about three years before moving to their home on Fork Mountain. Other than a brief move to Spruce Creek, Martha has lived on Fork Mountain ever since.

The Fitzgeralds had five children, and after Isaac died in June 1968, Martha married Wilfred Mays, who was also from Fork Mountain.

Martha on her porch

Snapdragons in an enamel pan on the porch

Martha's mountain home is filled with warmth and love, which shows on the smiling faces of the many family photographs gracing the walls. The day Margie Hatter and I came for the interview, we shared coffee and cake at the kitchen table, right next to a huge wood cook stove standing in the corner, which Martha says "gets its share of use, especially in the wintertime." The blackened cast-iron skillets

Martha (R) and her good friend Margie Hatter

hanging from the walls give the kitchen a lived-in look which cannot be duplicated in today's modern homes.

Martha speaks of her life along the Tye River and then on Fork Mountain as being a happy one. She says she has been blessed with all good neighbors because "there's a natural sweetness in the mountain people that you don't find elsewhere."

Martha Edward Phillips Fitzgerald Mays, who is still affectionately called "Marthy" by those who know her, is a perfect example of this sweetness, and I thanked her for letting us come into her home to share what life was like on the mountain in the early days.

Taken from the October 1988 *Backroads*

Protective cover on Marc Hite's "foot adze"

33

This 'n' That

Over the twenty-five years that *Backroads* newspaper was published, people were always sending in little articles that had an old-time flavor. I tried to print as many as I could, because they never failed to make me smile, and each was filled with a wealth of wisdom and nostalgia that people seemed to crave. Here are some of my favorites.

HOW THE MASON JAR GOT ITS NAME

Way back before the War between the States (there wasn't anything civil about it), some engineers were hired to lay out some boundaries. Two of the most important men who were doing this were a Mr. Mason and a Mr. Dixon. They went across the country from west to east laying their line. Working way out in the woods, they got awfully thirsty at times. They were drinking out of two old jelly glasses that were just alike. Now Mr. Dixon was a real persnickety fella who was careful about not drinking after anyone else. So they were always arguing about which glass was whose and not spending too much time working.

One day their straw boss had enough. He called them over to talk. He said, "If'n you fellers don't quit worryin' about these here jelly glasses, we won't ever get finished with the line before the war starts! Now Dixey [he called Dixon "Dixey" because he liked the way it made his eyes bulge], you 'n' Mason throw them jelly glasses away. Here's a jar for Mason and a plain cup for you. Now git gone and git done!"

Well sir, sure enough, that did the trick. Before too long Mason and Dixon had their line drawn and the job done.

And if it weren't for the straw boss coming up with Mason's jar and Dixie's cup so we could tell the north from the south, we might all be eating Cream of Wheat instead of grits!

A HUNTING TALE

The last time that I went hunting out west I took along my old, *old* rifle. We went up on a high mountain to hunt sheep and wild goats. The old timer that went with me took along a bag of salt. We saw a ram on the next ridge. The old timer told me to sit tight. He took a little drill from his pocket and drilled out some lead from a bullet and poured in some salt. Then he said, "Stand back and take notice." I said okay. He then stuck the bullet into my old rifle and took a long aim. He figured the distance and the wind blowing. Then he squeezed the trigger and set back to watch. After about twelve minutes the bullet hit the ram, and down he fell. We watched where the ram fell, and we started out. It took two weeks to get there. When we finally found him, he was already salted and cured! Now when I go hunting, I always use salted bullets. That way when I shoot some game and can't find it for a while, the meat will not spoil.

BURMA SHAVE

Are you old enough to remember the little signs that dotted the countryside along the back roads? As a girl, I loved reading the verses that accompanied the Burma Shave signs and made my dad slow down whenever we'd spot them. For all you youngsters out there, Burma Shave was a men's foaming shaving cream, and its advertisers thought these roadside testimonials would make their product more noticeable to the public. Here are a few of the limericks that were part of all us Baby Boomers' childhoods.

Going past schoolhouses
Take it slow
Let the little
Shavers grow
BURMA SHAVE

Late risers shave
In two minutes flat
Kiss your wife
And grab your hat
BURMA SHAVE

Within this vale
Of toil and sin
Your head grows bald
But not your chin
BURMA SHAVE

If these signs blur
And bounce around
You'd better park
And walk to town
BURMA SHAVE

Missin' Kissin'?
Perhaps your thrush

Can't get through
The underbrush
BURMA SHAVE

Every day
We do our part
To make your face
A work of art
BURMA SHAVE

YOU KNOW YOU'RE IN A SMALL TOWN

You know you're in a small town when . . .

- Fourth Street is on the edge of town
- You don't use your turn signal because everyone knows where you're going anyway
- You get run off Main Street by a combine
- You dial the wrong number and end up talking for fifteen minutes
- You write a check on the wrong bank and the folks there cover it for you
- The pickup trucks outnumber the cars three to one
- You miss a Sunday at church and receive a get-well card
- Someone asks you how you are and then *listens* to what you say

THE FUTURE AS SEEN IN 1950

- "I'll tell you one thing, if things keep going the way they are, it's going to be impossible to buy a week's worth of groceries for twenty dollars."

- "Did you hear the post office is thinking about charging a dime just to mail a letter?"

- "Have you seen the new cars coming out next year? It won't be long until $5,000 will only buy a used one."

- "Kids today are impossible. Those duck tail haircuts make it impossible to stay groomed. The next thing you know, boys will be wearing their hair as long as the girls."

- "If they raise the minimum wage to $1.00, nobody will be able to hire outside help at the stores."

- "Have you heard that the new church in town is allowing women to wear slacks to their services?"

WHAT MY MOTHER TAUGHT ME

My mother taught me to *Appreciate a Job Well Done:* "If you are going to kill each other, do it outside; I just finished cleaning!"

My mother taught me *Religion:* "You'd better pray that will come out of the carpet."

My mother taught me about *Time Travel:* "If you don't straighten up, I'm going to knock you into the middle of next week!"

My mother taught me *Logic:* "Because I said so, that's why."

My mother taught me *Irony:* "Keep crying, and I'll give you something to cry about."

My mother taught me about the science of *Osmosis:* "Shut your mouth and eat your supper."

My mother taught me about *Contortionism:* "Will you *look* at the dirt on the back of your neck!"

My mother taught me *Stamina:* "You'll sit there until all that spinach is finished."

My mother taught me about *Weather:* "It looks like a tornado swept through your room."

My mother taught me about *Hypocrisy:* "If I've told you once, I've told you a million times: Don't Exaggerate!"

My mother taught me about *Impossibility:* "If you fall out of that tree and break your leg, don't come running to me."

HOW TO MAKE HOME BREW

Chase wild bullfrogs fer three miles to gather up hops.

Add them to ten gallons of tan bark, ½ pint of shellac, and one bar of lye soap.

Boil thirty-six hours.

Strain through an I.W.W. sock to keep it from workin'.

Add one grasshopper to each pint to give it some kick.

Pour a little in the kitchen sink; if it takes the enamel off, it's ready to bottle.

SAD OBITUARY

It is with the saddest heart that I must pass on the following news. Please join me in remembering a great icon of the entertainment community.

The Pillsbury Doughboy died yesterday of a yeast infection and complications from repeated pokes in the belly. He was seventy-one years of age.

Doughboy was buried in a lightly greased coffin. Dozens of celebrities turned out to pay their respects, including Mrs. Butterworth, Hungry Jack, the California Raisins, Betty Crocker, the Hostess Twinkies, and Captain Crunch.

The gravesite was piled high with flours. Aunt Jemima delivered the eulogy and lovingly described Doughboy as a man who never knew how much he was kneaded. Doughboy rose quickly in show business, but his later life was filled with turnovers. He was not considered a very smart cookie, wasting much of his dough on half-baked schemes. Despite being a little flaky at times, he still, as a crusty old man, was considered a roll model for millions.

Doughboy is survived by his wife, Play Dough; two children, John Dough and Jane Dough; plus they had one in the oven. He is also survived by his elderly father, Pop Tart.

The funeral was held at 3:50 for about 20 minutes.

GRANDMA'S APRON

The principle use of Grandma's apron was to protect the dress underneath, but along with that, it served as a holder for removing hot pans from the oven; it was wonderful for drying children's tears; and on occasion, it was even used for cleaning out dirty ears. From the chicken coop, the apron was used for carrying eggs, fussy chicks, and sometimes half-hatched eggs to be finished in the warming oven over the kitchen wood cook stove.

When company came, those aprons were ideal hiding places for shy kids and when the weather was cold, Grandma wrapped it around her arms. Those big old aprons wiped many a perspiring brow, bent over the hot wood cook stove. Chips and kindling wood were brought into the kitchen in that apron.

From the garden, it carried all sorts of vegetables. After the peas had been shelled, it carried out the hulls. In the fall, the apron was used to bring in apples that had fallen from the trees. When unexpected company drove up the road, it was surprising how much furniture that old apron could dust in a matter of seconds. When dinner was ready, Grandma walked out on the porch, waved her apron, and the men knew it was time to come in from the fields to eat.

It will be a long time before someone invents something to replace that old-time apron that served so many purposes.

WACKY WEATHER FORECASTS

These old folklore weather predictions, humorous as they are, have solid, scientific backing to them and usually prove to be true.

A sun-shiny shower won't last a half an hour.

The evening red and the morning gray;
Is the sign of a bright and cheery day.
The evening gray and the morning red;
Put on your hat or you'll wet your head.

Red skies in the morning;
Sailors take warning.
Red skies at night;
Sailor's delight.

When the night has a fever,
It cries in the morning.

Rain before seven,
Clear before eleven.

Smells are stronger right before a storm
because of the drop in air pressure.

If you are without a thermometer and want to know how hot it is, just count a cricket's chirps for 15 seconds and add 37.

If the smoke from your campfire goes straight up,
expect good weather. If it curls downward, look out.

Birds perching more than usual are a sign of an oncoming storm
because flying is more difficult when air pressure drops.

If clouds are high in the sky they will produce rain,
but low clouds usually won't.

If there's dew on the grass at night then a good day is coming.
Dew forms only when the sky is clear and the air dry.

Wondering about humidity? Remember this jingle: "When the
glowworm lights his lamp, then the air is always damp."

OVER A HUNDRED YEARS AGO

Here are some statistics from 1902 that will make us think what
a difference a century makes!

- Average life expectancy in the United States was forty-seven years

- Only 14 percent of the homes in the U.S. had a bathtub
- Only 8 percent of the homes had a telephone
- A three-minute call from Denver to New York cost $11.00
- There were only 8,000 cars in America and only 144 miles of paved roads
- Maximum speed limit in most cities was 10 MPH
- Alabama, Mississippi, Iowa, and Tennessee were each more heavily populated than California
- The tallest structure in the world was the Eiffel Tower
- The average wage in the United States was twenty-two cents an hour
- More than 95 percent of all births took place in the home
- Sugar cost four cents a pound; eggs were fourteen cents a dozen; coffee was fifteen cents a pound
- Canada passed a law prohibiting poor people from entering the country for any reason
- The population of Las Vegas, Nevada, was thirty
- Crossword puzzles, canned beer, and iced tea hadn't even been thought of yet
- There was no Mother's Day or Father's Day
- Only 6 percent of all Americans graduated from high school
- There were only about 230 reported murders in the entire United States

Granny's Biscuit Bowl

A cypress tree of long ago
Gave us its lofty soul,

A sturdy gift of fine grain
For Grandmother's biscuit bowl.

The wood was carefully shaped
Contours smoothly sanded,
To form a shallow stirring place
That pleased the nimble-handed.

This bowl was daily dusted
By pyramids of flour,
And tasty biscuits were made
To bake for the dinner hour.

Now but a family heirloom
Its many scars attest,
And quietly speak of olden days
When Gran's biscuits were the best.

A LETTER FROM AUNT EFFIE

Lonesome Pine, N.C.
November 28, 1941

Dear Nephew,
Your uncle has a job at last! The first he has worked in forty-eight years.

We are rich now . . . $17.25 every Thursday. So we sent to Sears Roebuck for one of them new-fangled bathrooms like the rich people up north have.

You should see it. Over on one side of the room is a big, long white thing like the pigs drink out of. Only you can get in it, and take a bath all over. On the other side of the room is a little white gadget called a sink. This is for light washing; hands and face.

But over in the corner, Wow! There is a thing you can put one foot in and scrub until it gets clean then you pull a chain and you get fresh water for the other foot! They even sent us a roll of writing paper.

Yours Lovingly,
Aunt Effie

P.S. Two lids came with the darn thing but we ain't had any use for them, so I am using one for a bread board, and we framed Grandpa's picture in the other.

GREAT QUOTE

Lady Astor quite frankly said to Winston Churchill, "Sir, if you were my husband, I would poison your coffee."

Mr. Churchill responded, "Madam, if you were my wife, I'd drink it."

BACKROADS JOKE

He had taken his fiancée of eight years out to dinner.

As he was ordering, he asked her, "How would you like your rice?"

"Thrown," she replied.

MOUNTAIN MOTTO

"Eat it up, wear it out,
Make it do, or do without!"

Ralph and Doris Cash; Montebello, Virginia

Lynn hand washing clothes at her outdoor Laundromat

Courtesy of Charlotte Hodge

34

Scrub-Board Washing

When I was single and living in an old hunting camp that I rented here in Love, there was no place for a washing machine, which was just as well since I didn't have any money to buy one anyway. The thought of spending precious quarters, as well as my time, at the Laundromat twenty miles away didn't appeal to me in the least, so I invested in an old-fashioned washboard on which to scrub my clothes. All the older women I interviewed said it was how they used to do their laundry, so I figured I'd give it a try. It turned out to be quite an experience, and it gave me new appreciation for the hardships these women faced in their early lives. The following is an account of how I learned, by trial and error, to get clothes clean on a wooden washboard.

All the women I'd interviewed for *Backroads* gave me a heads up on how they used to do their wash, so I had somewhat of an idea before I started. They began by building a fire under a large iron kettle to boil the clothes in and had a supply of good old lye soap to get the dirt out. Not wanting to go back quite that far, I made a trip to the Farm Bureau and purchased a brand-new wood and glass "Crystal Cascade" scrub board, along with two galvanized washtubs, and headed for home. I reasoned that during the spring, summer, and fall months, I could do my laundry outside and string a line through the trees on which to dry my clothes. In winter, I'd move the scrubbing operation into the camp's shower and hang the clothes around the woodstove in the living room.

May 30, 1990, marked the starting date for my first attempt at backyard washing. I enlisted the help of my good friend Charlotte Hodge, who took all the photographs of the laundry process. We about died laughing trying to get the sequence correct and watching as I got soaked, but we persevered and in the end, we were successful.

Awkwardness was the theme of the day until I got the hang of handling the washboard, which, by the way, is not as easy as you'd think. Luckily, I had the perfect location for hand laundering: a cabin situated right next to the clear waters of Back Creek and an ever-flowing spring just out the back door. I cheated somewhat by boiling several large pots of water on my kitchen stove and mixing them with the cold spring water for a warm-water wash.

Since the washtub was sitting on the ground, I kind of "hunkered" over it, trying to balance myself and the scrub board at the same time. I knew at once that this was not going to work because my knees kept telling me so. I spotted the remains of an old treadle Singer sewing machine in the woods and with Charlotte's help, dragged the machine over to where I was washing and added a wide board across the top on which to set the tub. The other tub was left on the ground and filled with cold water and fabric softener for the "rinse cycle."

After I poured in the water, I squeezed in some Ivory Liquid and swished it around. I also had bar of Octagon soap, a small brush for scrubbing collars, and a spray bottle of diluted bleach for stubborn stains on my "whites," which I did first. That way, if some of the colored clothes bled in the water, it wouldn't matter.

I found I could use the wash board two different ways: leaning it against my chest and scrubbing with an up/down motion or propping it against the tub, using a back and forth action. Either way, it gets the clothes clean! But it takes a bit of practice to get used to the board itself and not skin your knuckles on the rippled edge of the glass.

I washed quite a bit of white clothing before hand-squeezing each piece and placing it in the rinse water. After soaking, I try not to "wring" the clothes too tight since it sets in the wrinkles. I found if I gently but firmly squeezed out the excess water before hanging up the clothes, they will dry smooth. They take a little longer to dry this way, but once they're hung, what are a few more hours? Between the fabric softener and the sunshine, your clothes smell so good when you bring them in from the line.

Materials gathered and ready to start

Gettin' down to business

Wringing out the clothes

Adding softener to the rinse water

Out of the rinse cycle . . .

. . . to the "solar dryer"

After the whites, I started in on my colored clothing in the same way. I found the hardest things to hand wash were my blue jeans and sheets. What a task! The jeans seem to get heavier and heavier as you scrub, but after a while you get a certain rhythm going, and it becomes easier. Actually, the whole process is rather therapeutic; you work along, letting your mind wander as it will. Sheets are the most cumbersome, and it feels like they grow in the wash water. I have to laugh at myself, wrestling the bulk of my Cannon percales. I found a way to minimize their size by folding them in two after they are rinsed and hanging them up on the line that way. When you take them down, they are already nicely folded.

After doing my clothes in this fashion for a while, I learned some valuable lessons. Number one is to make sure your clothes-line is tied off tight. I learned the hard way when hanging my last pair of heavy jeans and watching the whole line sag onto the ground, necessitating a rewash. I never made *that* mistake again! Number two is not to hurry, or scraped knuckles will result. The first time I washed, I got a wet stomach during the operation. The second time, I wore my bathing suit, a pair of cutoff Levi's, and my farm boots. This ensemble looked a bit strange but was working out nicely until the census taker came up unannounced and gawked at me.

There you have it, Lynn's adventure in hand scrubbing. So far it's worked out great, and I have only had to hit the Laundromat once during a rainy spell. Oh how I hated spending those quarters!

After this article appeared in the August 1990 issue of *Backroads*, Mr. W. P. Hite of Shacklefords, Virginia, sent this early newspaper clipping to me, which I've included for everyone's enjoyment.

"RECEET" FOR WASHING CLOTHES

1. Bild fire in backyard to heet kettle of rane water.
2. Set tubs so smoak won't blow in eyes if wind is pert.
3. Shave one hole cake lye soap in billin' water.
4. Sort things. Make three piles. One pile white, one pile cullord, one pile werk britches and rags.
5. Stur flowr in cold water to smooth then thin down with billin' water.
6. Rub durty spots on board and scrub hard. Then bile. Rub cullords but don't bile. Just rench and starch.
7. Take white things out of kettle with broom handel. Rench, blue, and starch.
8. Sprad tee towels on grass.
9. Hang old rags on fense.
10. Pore rench water in flowr bed.
11. Scrub porch with hot sopey water.

12. Turn tubs upside down.

13. Go put on a clean dress, smooth hair with side comb, brew up a batch of tee, and rest and rock a spell and count yore blessings.

Thelma McGann with her ever–present smile

35

Thelma Small McGann

Nellysford, Virginia

L ike so many of the mountain people, Thelma has lived all of her eighty-four years in the same location and says she wouldn't want to be anywhere else.

Born the first child and only daughter of Carl Elmore Small and his wife Fleetie Bradley Small, Thelma came into the world on September 19, 1917. She and her two younger brothers, Charles Glenroy and Carl Elwood, were raised in the family home about a half mile behind the present Valley Green Shopping Center in Nellysford.

Thelma's paternal grandparents were Adolphius Glenroy Small, whom everyone called "Doll," and Nannie Henderson Small. Her maternal grandparents were Henry Bradley and Minnie Miller Bradley.

Thelma's mama stayed at home nurturing her three children and ran the household while her husband Carl operated a sawmill where they lived. "Dad was a sawmill and log man," recalled Thelma. "He owned and operated his own mill and cut wood and sold lumber to the area people."

As a child, Thelma's mama instilled the love of domestic activities in her only daughter, which carried on throughout her life. Thelma loved cooking, cleaning, and decorating the house, but she loved sewing more than anything else. "I never was an outdoors woman. I was perfectly content to be inside doing housework.

An early Small family portrait, with Thelma in her mother's arms at top right

Daddy kind of pampered me and would give me money to go to John Goodwin's store to buy a length of pretty material. I'd go home and make a dress to wear to school the very next day."

In later years, Thelma continued these activities by cooking at her children's school, cleaning other people's houses from Nellysford to Afton, taking in sewing, hanging wallpaper, and painting. Thelma laughs when she says, "I reckon I've papered a room in every house in Nellysford at one time or another." At one time in her life, she cleaned house for seven different families, saying she loved seeing how pretty she could make them.

As a child, Thelma walked from her home to attend the Rockfish School. She remembers Miss Katie Dawson as one of her first teachers. Miss Dawson wore a large class ring on her finger, and when the children talked out of turn, she'd rap them on the head with it. Always a talker, Thelma said she thinks she still has a knot up there. Another teacher, Miss May, stood out in her mind because one time when some of the older children misbehaved, she brought a pistol to school. The foolishness abruptly stopped!

Thelma's five closest friends from childhood were Hilda Puckett, Ellen "Snip" Davis, Trosy and Louise Truslow, and Daisy Allen, whose family lived in the last house up on Spruce Creek. "If I wasn't at one of their houses, they were at mine. We'd walk a long ways just to see each other and talk . . . mostly about boys!"

Families who lived in the Nellysford area when Thelma was growing up were the Phillipses, Fitzgeralds, Truslows, Thompsons, Smalls, McGanns, Dodds, Hugheses, and a few Colemans. She remembers that "there were more Hugheses and Fitzgeralds than there were the rest of the people, and no end to the Smalls."

There were several general stores in the Nellysford area when Thelma was young: John Goodwin's Mercantile, the store that Forest Hughes ran, Small's Store, and one operated by the Dodd family. Now all that's left of those stores are the memories.

Thelma said she stayed in school to the eighth grade, and "by then I was so smart, I married Willard McGann." Willard was two years and two weeks older than Thelma. She had grown up with him her whole life, but she began noticing him noticing *her* when she was fourteen years old. They married when she was just fifteen years of age. Thelma said her husband was just "naturally smart." "He could sit down and read the newspaper and then tell you, word for word, what it said. Years after he left school, he could still name the capitals of every state in the union." At first, Willard worked at the sawmill that Thelma's daddy owned but later got a job in Waynesboro at Wayne Manufacturing.

The young couple was married on August 8, 1934, at the Methodist parsonage in Lovingston by a preacher named Abernathy. Thelma wore a light-blue dress with white lace at the yoke and a large white hat. Willard, whom his bride thought was the handsomest man she'd ever met, wore a dark suit. Willard's brother-in-law drove them to Lovingston, and both mothers attended their children's wedding. Thelma recollects that people used to say that they were the best-looking couple in Nelson County. After the ceremony, the couple went back to Willard's

The McGann homeplace

parents' home. They lived there for two years before Thelma's daddy had a three-room house built for them just up the road from where they lived on Spruce Creek. By this time, two of their six children had been born, brought into the world by Thelma's mother-in-law, Lovie McGann, who was a midwife.

They lived there for eight years before buying a three-room log cabin built by Charlie Dameron, just down the road from their former home. The McGanns tore down the old home and used the lumber to build an addition onto the cabin. This new addition provided another bedroom, a dining room, and a porch. Willard and Thelma worked hard, adding sheetrock to the inside, along with many other improvements. It was a warm and cozy place, a safe haven for their growing family.

By 1945, the McGanns had five sons: Jimmy, Carl, Donald, Freddie, and Danny. At this point, Willard went into the military. Before he left, he bought a Chevrolet truck so that he could teach his wife to drive. One trip down Old Stoney Creek Road, with chickens flying in every direction, convinced Willard he didn't have the nerve to continue the driving lessons. He told Thelma that if she wanted to drive, she'd have to teach herself. And that's

Thelma and Willard with five of their children

just what she did! Leaving the boys with Mrs. McGann, Thelma would bump up and down the road in that old truck, learning to shift gears with the best of them.

Willard was gone for one year. After he returned, their last child and only daughter, Phyllis, was born. While working at Wayne Manufacturing, Willard brought home twenty-eight dollars a week, which Thelma said they lived better on than some do now. "Willard would give me money to buy what we needed, and his paycheck went a lot further than you'd think. I still have the same furniture today that I bought when we got married. Back then, I bought two oak rocking chairs for five dollars. Now you couldn't replace the same type of chair for hundreds of dollars."

When Phyllis started school, Thelma went to work, taking a cooking job at the Rockfish Valley School where the children attended. She stayed at that job for twenty-one years. After that, she became a cook at the Tuckahoe Tavern. Her son Donald says his mother is such a good cook that crackers march right on up to their house just to jump in her homemade vegetable soup! The McGanns always had a large garden to feed their family. Thelma said that she must have canned thousands of quarts of food in her lifetime.

Thelma said their home was always full of activity with six children underfoot, but they had a lot of fun. "We had enough kids that they could get a ball game going and didn't need anyone else to play. And you've never seen anything like how much five grown boys could eat. There was never a dull moment at the McGann house!"

Willard died suddenly on August 11, 1982, while helping his wife plant the garden. At the time, he

Thelma and Willard on their forty-seventh wedding anniversary

was employed at a lumber yard in Crozet. It was exactly one year and three days after he and Thelma had celebrated their forty-seventh wedding anniversary. Thelma continued to live in the home she and Willard had made together until three years ago, when the decision was made to make a move into a new modular home directly in back of their old homeplace. She continues to enjoy sewing, and her daughter, Phyllis, keeps her supplied with throwaway cameras that Thelma uses to take pictures of everyone who comes to visit. Her sons and daughter take care of all her needs, and she says they have all been good children.

In addition to her own children, Thelma now has twenty-two grandchildren, thirty-six great-grandchildren, and six great-great-grandchildren. All live in the surrounding area except her son Jimmy's boy, who is stationed in Georgia with his family. Her grandson Jeff has written several songs that are now being played on WKDW, a Staunton radio station.

When asked how things in the Nellysford area have changed in the last eighty-four years, Thelma is quick to answer. "At one time or another, everyone here was either my aunt, uncle, or cousin. I

All six of the McGann children in later years

was kin to nearly everyone here. Back when I was growing up, everyone knew everybody, and there was a lot of visiting in homes. I'd set out on the porch swing and wave to the folks going by. Times were a lot harder when I grew up, but you never had to worry, never had to lock your doors, because people could be trusted. You can ask anyone in Nelson County, and they all know Thelma McGann. I've lived here all my life and wouldn't want to be anywhere else."

Taken from the June 2002 *Backroads*

Irvin and Melba Rosen in 2004 after their sixty-seventh wedding anniversary

36

Irvin and Melba Rosen

McKinley, Virginia

I n all the years I wrote stories for *Backroads*, there was one man who possessed the most God-given talents of anyone I ever knew. That man was Irvin Rosen. I don't exactly remember when we first talked, but most likely he called to tell me about an obscure tool that I could feature in the "What Is It" column of the paper. From that time on, he called frequently, asking if I'd like to come out to his McKinley home to watch and record an old-time activity. Irvin was responsible for the preservation of many traditional crafts that would otherwise have gone quietly by the wayside. Those of us privileged to know him realized we were in the presence of greatness, yet his humble, quiet demeanor drew you to him and made you feel comfortable in his company.

Because of Irvin's diverse knowledge, this chapter will have several parts, starting with Irvin and his sweet wife, Melba, who was the perfect compliment to her husband. When the photo to the left was taken in July 2004, the Rosens had just celebrated their sixty-seventh wedding anniversary, and along with that picture I printed a brief history of their lives. Next, Irvin demonstrates how to correctly graft a fruit tree and shows us his antique tool collection and the history behind the tools.

First and foremost, Irvin was a master clockmaker, and, ironically enough, it is the one thing I never interviewed him about. Irvin's amazing talent wasn't limited to just a few things. He was a competent carpenter, building beautiful pieces of heirloom furniture for his family and friends. He was one of those rare men who could look at problem and solve it after simply thinking about it for a while. But what impressed me most about Irvin and Melba Rosen was the fact they were both committed Christians, living out their faith in a quiet yet proactive way that never left a doubt as to what kind of folks they were. As of this writing, both Irvin and Melba have passed away, but in the following articles, both were living active and vital lives.

ROSENS CELEBRATE SIXTY-SEVENTH WEDDING ANNIVERSARY

July 18, 2004, marks a very special milestone for Irvin and Melba Rosen. It is the day of their sixty-seventh wedding anniversary.

Irvin Thomas Rosen, the youngest child of three and the only son of Finley H. Rosen and Sarah Virginia Hildebrand Rosen, was born on October 29, 1915, in the family home in McKinley, Virginia.

Melba Louise Hampton, the eldest daughter of five children born to Chancy Hampton and Eula Ruth Hampton, was born on November 5, 1915, in Grayson County, Virginia.

As a young woman, Melba was visiting in Staunton when she met her future husband, Irvin. They were married at the parsonage of Rev. David Glovier on July 18, 1937. The young couple, who were both twenty-two years old at the time of their marriage, lived with Irvin's parents for a time. A little two-room schoolhouse, located next door to Irvin's father's house, was vacant after the school was relocated, and Finley Rosen bought it. Together, he and Irvin remodeled the building, and when it was finished, the young couple moved in and called it home. The Rosens still reside in the warm and cozy home after all these years.

Irvin and Melba had two sons: Thomas Hampton, born on March 9, 1938, and Jerry Edward, born July 1, 1942. Tommy is married to Peggy, and they have one son. Jerry married Joyce, and they have two daughters and a son.

Irvin, an active and industrious man, has had many successful vocations in his eighty-nine years. Like his father before him, Irvin has built his share of houses, fine furniture, and has been a cabinet maker and builder of exquisite clocks during his lifetime. He also worked for thirty-one years at the Virginia School for the Deaf and Blind, starting in 1941 and retiring in the early 1970s.

Before marriage, Melba worked at the Montgomery Ward Company in Staunton. After her sons were born, however, she began her career as a full-time mother, nurturing her children in that special way a stay-at-home mom can. In the early 1940s, Melba began to have problems with her eyesight, and today she is considered legally blind.

But the Rosens are busy, active people, full of good humor and a zest for life that many envy. In addition to their two sons, they have four grandchildren and seven great-grandchildren, all of whom are their pride and joy.

In a world where long happy marriages are on the decline, we congratulate Irvin and Melba Rosen of McKinley, Virginia, who have just celebrated sixty-seven years together and have plans for many more anniversaries. May God's continued blessings be yours!

Taken from the August 2004 *Backroads*

ROSEN RESTORES FAMOUS FRIESIAN CLOCK

Anyone who has read the book *The Hiding Place* is familiar with the author, Corrie Ten Boom, and what she and her family were forced to endure when they were caught aiding the Jewish people during the Nazi regime.

In the first chapters of the book, a Friesian clock was lovingly referred to several times by the author, who had happy memories of growing up in the family home and watch shop in Haarlem, Holland.

This clock was a fixture in the Ten Boom family for almost 150 years, and it hung in the home where Corrie was apprenticed to her father as a certified watchmaker. Young Corrie was often reminded by her father "not to ever let the Friesian clock run down."

Never having married, Corrie was caretaker to most of her immediate family and also assisted in the efforts to help area Jews hide and escape Nazi persecution. Because of these efforts, the family was found out, and Corrie was sent to a concentration camp where she and many others were brutalized. She later wrote *The Hiding Place*, highlighting her experiences throughout that time. She also traveled the globe as an evangelical speaker and wrote several other books about her commitment to the Christian faith.

Recently, Rev. Bob Stamps and his wife Ellen, both of Richmond, were surprised to learn that they were the recipients of the Friesian clock. They hired Irvin to restore it to its former grandeur. Ellen, who is a native of the Netherlands, served as Corrie Ten Boom's secretary for nine years as she traveled the world before her death in 1983. The clock was shipped from Holland to Rev. and Mrs. Stamps in a large wooden crate, carefully packed to insure the antique's safety.

So that's how the famous Friesian clock miraculously found its way from the Ten Boom

Irvin poses next to the famous Friesian clock that he restored

Clock Shop to National Association of Watch and Clock Collectors member Irvin Rosen's Clock Shop in McKinley, Virginia.

The six-foot-long clock was given new side and bottom veneer, as well as new beadwork around the clock face. Irvin also replaced the glass on the bottom port hole located on the front of the timepiece. The dial, which had flaked, also had to be restored, and Irvin sent the piece to Georgia where the historic scenery was repainted on the top and corner pieces of the dial. He said a clock of this type, which is thought to have been made by clockmaker G. Boorsma in 1856, would be worth around six thousand dollars on today's market.

Thanks to the efforts and clock-making talent of Irvin Rosen, Corrie Ten Boom's Friesian masterpiece will once again be treasured and hung for all to see and appreciate.

Taken from the December 2004 *Backroads*

GRAFTING FRUIT TREES

Grafting is an ancient horticultural process in which a part of one plant is united with another without having a root system of its own. A "scion," which is the budding stem of a desired tree, is inserted into a stock of another, which alters the "host" plant's character by modifying the fruit produced on that tree. It can enhance defective or poorly producing trees, or as Irvin Rosen says, "Grafting is the art of getting something good for nothing!"

Irvin invited Billy and me to come out to his McKinley home and watch him graft some apple trees to learn how the grafting technique works.

Grafting has got to be done in the early spring while the scions are still in their dormant stage, before the buds begin to swell. He says that early apples such as Early Harvest, Lodi, and Early Transparent are the easiest to graft and have the best success rate. The scions to be cut and used must be taken from last year's growth and should have at least two buds on it. In the following photographs,

Irvin demonstrates the six basic steps of grafting. First find a desirable scion to graft into a less-desirable tree stock. Then taper down the scion with a knife to enable it to fit into the stock. The scion Irvin was using the day we came had been cut around the first of March and kept dormant in the refrigerator until needed. Next, a seedling must be found to graft onto. Irvin cut the stock of an undesirable seedling that had come up in his yard, then took his grafting knife, called a cleft grafting tool, and cut a

Irvin showing a grafted tree

slot across the center of the stock. Into this slot, two tapered scions were inserted at either side and masking tape was applied to both the stock and bottom of the scions. This is to keep them from drying out. Irvin said his father used to use wax, but he has found the tape works just as well.

When warm weather comes, the grafted scions, drawing their nourishment from their new parent root stock, begin to bud and bloom. The last photo above shows a tree Irvin had grafted two years previously. Notice how the new limbs have twined around their adoptive stock, making it all one tree. Grafting makes it possible to have a Red Delicious apple stock which produces a Stayman or Yellow Delicious apple.

Taken from the May 1995 *Backroads*

A scion cut from a desired tree

Tapering down the scion

Cutting the seedling that will take the graft

A grafting knife is used for splitting the seedling

The tapered end of the scion is inserted in the tree stock, and masking tape is applied

Two years' growth on a previously grafted tree

FOR THE LOVE OF ANTIQUE TOOLS

In July 1994, Irvin Rosen called to ask if my husband and I were interested in seeing his collection of antique tools and the small museum he housed them in at his McKinley home. This is possibly the first time we had met face to face, although we had talked on the phone numerous times. I did a *Backroads* auto tour through the Middlebrook area in 1988 and remember seeing a sign that said, "'Its About Time,' Irvin Rosen, Clock Maker." I always meant to come back for a story but somehow never followed up on it. So we were delighted when he called and quickly took him up on the offer to see his collection of early tools.

Upon arrival, we were privileged to get a tour of Irvin's clock workshop and see firsthand the intricate tools used to build his clocks. Drawers of wooden inlays and decorative moldings held the contents of his world-renowned timepieces. He showed us some beautifully detailed trim with a pie-crust ripple effect that had become obsolete. Irvin, not wanting to see it disappear, invented a machine to duplicate the old trim. He now uses it on many of the one-of-a-kind clocks he is commissioned to build by people who want an heirloom for the future. We were completely speechless when, at the end of our visit, Irvin presented us with a small handmade clock that today graces our cabin.

Walking into the backyard museum was a feast to a carpenter's eyes. Walls, floors, and benches were filled with every conceivable antique hand tool you could imagine. A wealth of wooden hand planes, mortising gauges, pump drills, a hand-cranked lathe, a foot-powered "Velocipede" scroll saw (or "jig saw"), tap wrenches, axes, and saws made up just a small portion of his inventory.

The most amazing thing about Irvin's collection is that the majority of the tools were inherited from his ancestors. There aren't many people who can say they have their great-grandfather's tools, from both sides of the family. In fact, Irvin also has the records of his great-grandfather, Dave Berry, who was a cabinet-maker in the 1800s. Mr. Berry also made coffins for local people, and one entry of his bill book, dated 1858, stated: "One neat coffin and plans for grave, $5.50. Use of hearse to haul to grave, $1.00." Another said, "Coffin for little daughter, .87 and one-half cent."

Irvin peddling the "Velocipede"

Irvin's mother inherited all of her grandfather Berry's tools when he passed away, and she, in turn, passed them on to her only son. The rest of the family, knowing Irvin's love for old tools, followed suit and are happy to know their keepsakes are carefully preserved, appreciated, and displayed at his home.

When asked when he formally started collecting, Irvin laughed and said, "It's sort of like asking when I started attending the church down here . . . I can't remember when I didn't! I guess I've always had a fascination for tools and every one available that I can afford, I try to buy." I asked if his collection was now complete or if he would keep adding to it. Irvin emphatically said he'd keep on collecting. "Why, I've gone to an auction and waited all day just to bid on one certain tool I wanted." Irvin said he wouldn't enjoy his collection nearly as much if he couldn't show it off to others who have an appreciation of fine hand tools. My next question was inevitable: Will you pass them on to anyone in your family that loves them as much as you do? I was relieved to hear that both of his sons and their families share the love and respect for the old tools, and they will be passed on to the next generation.

Some of the tools in Irvin's collection

Looking at a rather large tool that resembled a spinning wheel, Irvin explained that it was a hand-cranked lathe. He gave us a demonstration of how the lathe worked and told us a story about a particular candle stand that was made on it. When he was fifteen years old, Irvin and his father made their first tilt-top candle stand on the lathe and several other pieces of small household items. They took them to a community fair for display purposes and ended up selling the candle stand for five dollars. Irvin kept up with the whereabouts of that particular piece, which made its way to South Carolina, and several years ago bought it back to put in his museum for the whopping price of $300.00.

He showed us a tool used for cutting tongue-and-groove flooring, a Stanley combination plane that was in excellent condition and still fully functional.

Irvin's favorite tool is one he made himself. It is called a pump drill and operates on the "button on a string" principle. He said this type of tool is very rare and even if you could find one, it would be out of the ordinary person's price range. The drill cannot be used on the wall or ceiling because of the way it operates, but on the floor or any other type of flat surface, it really does the job.

A Stanley combination plane for tongue-and-groove work

After showing us several types of wooden planes, Irvin let Billy shave a portion of ornate molding that was lying on his work-bench. It was something to see a tool so simple produce something so beautiful. Irvin laughed as he told Billy, "And if I get enough visitors, I get my molding made!"

Taken from the
August 1994 *Backroads*

A pump drill that Irvin built

Raymond Oliver; Tyro, Virgina

Ancestors

Your tombstone stands among the rest,
Neglected and alone,
The name and date are chiseled out,
On polished marble stone.

It reaches out to all who care,
It is too late to mourn.
You did not know that I exist.
You died and I was born.

Yet each of us are cells of you,
In flesh, in blood, in bone.
Our blood contracts and beats a pulse,
Entirely not our own.

Dear Ancestor, the place you filled,
So many years ago.
Spreads out among the ones you left,
Who would have loved you so.

I wonder if you lived and loved.
I wonder if you knew,
That someday I would find this spot,
And come to visit you.

About the Author

 Even as a child, Lynn Coffey had a Waldenish bent toward a nineteenth-century existence, despite the fact that she was growing up along the busy Gold Coast of southern Florida, with all the amenities of modern living. Her dream was to someday live in a log cabin in the mountains and live a quiet, self-sufficient lifestyle.

Lynn began living that dream upon moving to the tiny hamlet of Love, Virginia, in the summer of 1980. As she met and got to know her neighbors, all of whom were quite elderly at the time, she soon realized the culture of these hearty Scottish/Irish descendants was slowly vanishing and needed to be preserved.

Without any formal education or prior experience in journalism, Lynn carved out a folksy niche of documenting early Appalachian life through the pages of a monthly newspaper called *Backroads*, the first issue being published in December 1981. For the next twenty-five years, *Backroads* chronicled the history of the mountain people as Lynn traveled the hills and hollers, interviewing the elders and photographing handicrafts and activities that had been handed down for generations.

In the process, little did she realize how entwined their lives would become or how much the mountain people would come to mean to her as they opened their hearts to trust a young woman who started out as an "outsider" and ended up becoming one of them.

You can request additional copies of *Backroads 3* by using this order form.

ORDER FORM

Name _____

Address _____

City, State, Zip _____

Please send me _____ copies of *Backroads 3* at $20.00 each plus $5.00 per book shipping.

Make checks or money orders payable to Lynn Coffey and mail to:

Lynn Coffey
1461 Love Road
Lyndhurst, VA 22952
www.backroadsbooks.com